2

TEACHER'S EDITION

Focus on Phonics

SHORT VOWEL SOUNDS AND CONSONANT BLENDS

BY GAIL V. RICE

New Readers Press
ProLiteracy's publishing division

Focus on Phonics 2 Teacher's Edition
ISBN 978-1-56420-947-4

Copyright © 2011, 1991, 1982, 1980, 1979 New Readers Press
New Readers Press
ProLiteracy's Publishing Division
104 Marcellus Street, Syracuse, NY 13204
www.newreaderspress.com

Printed in the United States of America
9   8   7   6

Proceeds from the sale of New Readers Press materials support professional
development, training, and technical assistance programs of ProLiteracy
that benefit local literacy programs in the U.S. and around the globe.

Developmental Editor: Terrie Lipke
Creative Director: Andrea Woodbury
Production Specialist: Maryellen Casey
Art and Design Supervisor: James P. Wallace
Illustrations: Bill Peterson, Ron Mahoney, and Drew Rose, represented by Wilkinson Studios, Inc.
Cover Design: Carolyn Wallace

Table of Contents

II. Beginning Blends with *l*

III. Beginning Blends with *r*

IV. Beginning Blends with *s* and *w*

V. Beginning Three-letter Blends

VI. Review of Beginning Blends

VII. Ending Blends with *n*

VIII. Other Ending Blends

IX. Vowels + *r*

X. Reading Longer Words

XI. Story

XII. Appendixes

To the Teacher

Focus on Phonics 2: Short Vowel Sounds and Consonant Blends is a combination of two books that were previously published separately: *Focus on Phonics-2a: Short Vowel Sounds* and *Focus on Phonics-2b: Consonant Blends*. Part A of this book is correlated to *Laubach Way to Reading 2*. Part B on consonant blends gives additional help on beginning and ending consonant blends.

What is *Focus on Phonics*?

Focus on Phonics is a four-level (grade levels 0–4) series designed to increase a student's ability to read independently by applying word-attack skills to new words. It is also a comprehensive spelling program. Each level includes a teacher's edition and a student workbook with exercises to reinforce recognition of various sounds, letters, and words.

Focus on Phonics differs from traditional phonics approaches. Book 1 focuses on the sounds and names of the letters as both beginning and ending sounds in words. Books 2–4 use a word-pattern approach in which the regularities of spelling are emphasized. Instead of having to work with isolated sounds and syllables, students learn new words in a meaningful context. Sight words are introduced, and students learn to read and write not only new words but also complete sentences. The series covers all phonics elements and provides extensive practice with prefixes, suffixes, homonyms, compound words, and syllabication, with periodic reviews. The series is easier than other phonics materials because not many difficult multisyllable words are introduced until book 4. Thus, *Focus on Phonics* provides a solid foundation and eases the transition into other more fast-paced, difficult phonics materials.

Focus on Phonics is correlated to the skill books in *Laubach Way to Reading* and is a valuable supplement to that series. But *Focus on Phonics* can also be used on its own as a helpful phonics series that will fit into many reading programs. It is designed to be flexible. Depending on the needs of your student, you can start at any level or even skip over parts of books (the instructions give guidelines for this). You can work at whatever rate is best for your student. Some students may slow down and do only a few parts of a practice at one time. On the other hand, students with more reading or writing ability or those who only need a quick review of some sounds may save time by skipping over practices for sounds they already know well or doing only part of some practices. Some students can do sections of the *Focus on Phonics* practices on their own—you can easily make recordings to assist with this. And you can use *Focus on Phonics* with groups as well as with individuals. (See Appendix B, Using This Workbook with Groups.)

Even if you are using another phonics series as your core material, *Focus on Phonics* can be a helpful resource because it provides rather exhaustive word lists for all common word families and lists of compound words and homonyms. It also provides many useful exercises on common prefixes (beginnings) and suffixes (endings) added to root words. Also, the periodic reviews throughout the books can be used as diagnostic, placement, or evaluation tests.

What is the purpose of *Focus on Phonics*?

Workbook 2 assumes that students know individual consonant sounds very well, which will be necessary to decode words with short vowel sounds and consonant blends. It reinforces these sound-symbol relationships and helps the student build a foundation for sounding out and spelling new words with the short sounds for *a, e, i, o,* and *u.* (*Focus on Phonics 1: Sounds and Names of Letters* is excellent preparation for this book, but if the student knows those consonant sounds well, he may skip that book.) It also gives extensive practice with beginning and ending consonant blends.

Who should use *Focus on Phonics*?

Part A of *Focus on Phonics 2* is useful for students who may have been introduced to the letters and sounds in the corresponding *Laubach Way to Reading 2* lessons. It is also useful for those who are learning the vowel sounds for the first time, those who are reviewing them, and those who need practice in mastering those sound-symbol relationships and applying them to new words. Part B of this book is not correlated to any of the skill books but is often helpful to those using any reading and phonics programs because beginning and ending consonant blends are not usually covered in those programs in as much detail as they are in this book. *Focus on Phonics* (like *Laubach Way to Reading*) is designed for adults and older teenagers.

Focus on Phonics is especially ideal for students who are not primarily visual learners, who depend also on auditory or other methods. Students see, hear, say, and write words. The word-family approach that is used helps students learn groups of words easily by seeing and hearing their similarities and differences. And students are likely to remember the sound-symbol relationships because they are exposed to many words (in each family) to illustrate those relationships. Students see the reasons why words are spelled and pronounced as they are. The focus is not so much on remembering words, but on learning to figure out words—a great help for students whose visual memory is so poor that they forget words again and again after seeing them, and for students who are not able to generalize from a few key words to other new words. These skills help students to become independent learners who will not always need help or controlled-vocabulary materials.

Focus on Phonics is useful not only for beginners but also for remedial students reading at the second- to fourth-grade level who need intensive help in sound-symbol relationships. It can also serve students who have gaps in their knowledge or who have never had an explicit or sequential presentation of phonics.

v

Many students cannot spell words that they are able to read. Their spelling ability often lags behind their reading ability (sometimes by several grade levels). *Focus on Phonics* offers a complete spelling program in books 2–4 if students write out the words and sentences.

Focus on Phonics helps students increase their vocabulary as they discuss with you the meanings of the words used in the practices and their meanings as used in the sentences.

Focus on Phonics can be useful for many English-as-a-Second-Language (ESL) students if they have developed some real listening and speaking skills. To avoid overwhelming these students, you may want to skip over many words and concentrate on ones they can relate to with their limited listening and speaking vocabulary. They should know that they are not expected to remember the spellings of all the words they see or the meanings of all the words they hear or pronounce.

How to use the student workbook and teacher's edition

Part A of *Focus on Phonics 2* is correlated to *Laubach Way to Reading 2*. Each numbered practice of Part A in the student workbook corresponds to a lesson in the skill book. If you are using this book with *Laubach Way to Reading 2*, have the student read at least the key words and story of the skill book lesson (and any supplementary stories like *More Stories*, if desired) before doing any of the practices that correspond to that lesson. Because there are usually several practices for each skill book lesson in Part A (e.g., Practice 4-A, 4-B, 4-C for skill book lesson 4), your student may often lag behind in *Focus on Phonics* practices from where he is in the skill book lessons. In that case, you may want to review the key words in the skill book lesson before starting the corresponding *Focus on Phonics* practice. Students may not want to wait to finish Part B of this book before beginning *Laubach Way to Reading Skill Book 3* or *Focus on Phonics 3*, so they may be working simultaneously in Part B of this book and in those two books. You may need to help students with words that have consonant blends in *Focus on Phonics 3* if they have not finished Part B and have not covered those consonant blends before.

If you are *not* using Part A of this workbook with *Laubach Way to Reading*, then the words in part 1 and any "Review words" in part 5 of the regular short vowel practices may be new to your student. Teach them as new words when necessary.

The teacher's edition contains replicas of the practices in the student workbook, with the answers filled in. With the first practice of each type, step-by-step instructions are provided. You do not have to follow the suggested dialog exactly, but before doing a practice, you should become familiar with the instructions. The instructions are designed for one-to-one teaching but can be adapted for groups or classrooms. (See Appendix B.) The Appendixes provide additional word lists and other resources.

In the instructions, *T* stands for *Teacher* or *Tutor*, and *S* stands for *Student*. Slash marks around a letter or letters indicate the sound for which they stand. Slash marks around a vowel indicate the short sound of the vowel. Thus, you say /a/ like the vowel sound in *pan*. When you see slash marks around a consonant blend, such as /sn/ or /nd/, say the sounds rather than the letter names. Letters in italics are read by their letter names, as *a, b, c*. When words or parts of words are to be spelled out, they are hyphenated like this: *t-a-n*.

In each practice, speak slowly and clearly, repeating words if necessary. If it helps the student to repeat words after you, make sure he pronounces them correctly. Brief directions for each exercise in a practice are printed in both the student workbook and the teacher's edition. Read these directions aloud to the student. If there is a Note at the top of the regular short vowel or consonant blend practices, it gives directions for that practice only. In most cases, you will be working with the student, correcting each answer as he speaks or writes it. On some practices where the student can work alone (e.g., Reviews), you may want to check his work in a section after he has done one or two items to make sure that he understands the directions. Be sure that mistakes are corrected before the student goes on to the next practice. Adapt the workbook to each student by choosing how fast to go and which parts are necessary to cover.

Some words with short vowel sounds or consonant blends have been omitted from the word families. That is because this workbook includes only those words whose meanings are most commonly known, as determined by *The Living Word Vocabulary* by Edgar Dale and Joseph O'Rourke (Field Enterprises Educational Corporation, 1976). This national vocabulary inventory gives the meanings of words and the grade levels at which they are known.

Special problems

Students with dialects, foreign students, and those with speech problems may not give the standard pronunciation for all the sounds. (Not all English sounds exist in other languages.) For the purposes of this workbook, it is enough if students can hear the sounds when you say them, can identify the sounds with their letters, and can read words using their own pronunciation. Other students with great auditory or visual learning problems should be diagnosed and treated by specialists. They may require a more specialized approach than these materials can provide.

However, many students may struggle with blending sounds, decoding new words, and recognizing words in general because they do not have phonemic awareness skills. These skills are foundational and need to be developed before students can apply their knowledge of phonics. Some students who develop phonics skills struggle with reading anyway. Read Appendix A: Phonics, Phonemic Awareness, and the Process of Reading. This Appendix will help you understand the place of phonics in reading and how to develop phonemic awareness skills in students who don't have them.

Part A: Short Vowel Sounds

This section begins with the exercise "Do They Rhyme?" which introduces the concept of rhyming words to prepare the student for working with word families. "Two Forms of the Letter *a*" introduces the letter-form *a* for students who know only the form *a*. (In this workbook, the form *a* is used in the body type. Knowing both forms will help the student read a variety of printed and typewritten supplementary materials.)

Parts I–V, which cover the five short vowels, contain four types of practices: word families, adding endings, contrasting short vowels, and review. The word-family practices help the student apply his knowledge of short vowel words to new words that are similar in form. The student reads and spells several new words in the word family, reviews some skill book words, learns some new sight words, and reads meaningful sentences containing the new words. You may also have the student write all or some of the sentences.

The practices on adding endings deal with *-s*, *-ing*, *-ed*, and *-y*, introducing the skill of doubling the final consonant before adding the ending in one-syllable words. The student learns both to read and to spell words with these endings.

The practices on contrasting short vowels pair two vowels that may be confused and give the student practice in distinguishing words that contain those vowels.

Parts I–V each end with a review of words containing the short vowel being studied. Part VI covers adding the endings *-es* and *-er* to words and changing the final *y* to *i* before adding certain endings. Part VII gives the student practice reading both compound words and two-syllable words containing short vowels.

Note: Although we recognize that there are students of both sexes, for the sake of clarity and simplicity we chose to use the pronouns *he*, *him*, and *his* throughout this book when referring to a student.

Do They Rhyme?

This brief exercise introduces the concept of rhyming words. Begin by giving the student some examples of words that rhyme and words that don't. Say some pairs of words and have the student tell if they rhyme or not. Then introduce the exercise.

T. says: Look at the pictures and say the words. Do the words rhyme? Make a check in the box if they do.

Make sure that the student says the right words for the pictures and pronounces the words correctly.

Check the student's work when he has finished the exercise.

Then, go through the rhyming pairs. Ask the student if he can think of some *more* words that rhyme with each pair. Finally, ask him if he can think of some words that *do* rhyme with each of the remaining words.

If the student recognizes rhyming words and can rhyme words, he will probably be able to learn many words from the word-family approach used in this workbook.

Student's page 5

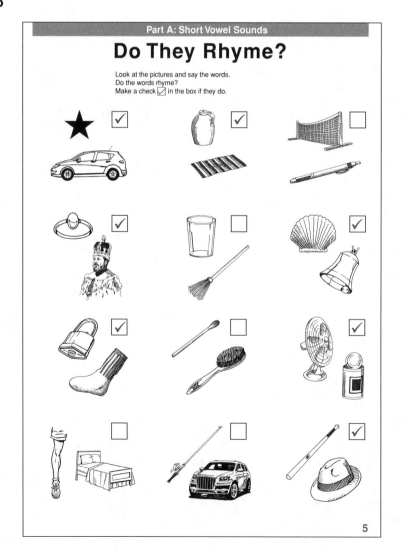

8

Two Forms of the Letter a

Teacher's Instructions

This exercise introduces the student to the letter-form a, which is used in this workbook. If the student has used only the form *a* up to now and is not familiar with the form a, have him do this exercise before he begins his workbook.

1 If the student is already familiar with both forms of the letter *a*, he can skip this exercise.

T. says: [Point to the letter **a** in the box.] This is the letter **a**.
You have seen this letter **a** in stories you have read.
And when you write the letter **a**, it looks like this.

[Point to the letter **a** in the box.] This letter is **a**, too.
It just looks a little different. This **a** is used in many books. It is used in this book.

But when you write the letter **a**, you will still write it like this **a**. [Point to the **a** in the box.]

T. says: [Point to **at** in the left column.] This word is **at**.
[Point to **at** in the right column.] This word is **at**, too.

Both words are spelled the same: a, t. The *a*'s are just a little different.

Go over the rest of the words with the student. Make sure he understands that the words are the same even though the *a*'s are different. Finally, have the student read all the words in both columns, first **at**, then **at**, and so on.

2 Circle all the words that are spelled the same as the first one.

T. says: Circle all the words that are spelled the same as the first one.

Check the student's work. Make sure he recognizes words that are spelled the same but have different forms of the letter *a*.

3 Write these words.

T. says: These words have the new letter *a*. [Point to the first word, **an**.]
Read each word and then write it on the line. Write the *a* the same way you have written it before, like this.
[Point to the **an** written on the first line.]

Make sure the student writes the **a** correctly in each word.

4 Read these sentences.

T. says: In these sentences, you will see the new letter **a**.
Read these sentences.

If the student still has trouble recognizing the new letter **a** when he has completed this exercise, you may need to make up more exercises similar to these to help him.

9

Two Forms of the Letter **a**

Two Forms of the Letter **a**

1.

| **a** | **=** | **a** |

at   at
and and
man man
has has

2. Circle all the words that are spelled the same as the first one.

an	(an)	on	(an)	in	and	(an)
are	and	(are)	an	(are)	at	(are)
at	(at)	in	(at)	is	on	(at)
has	his	(has)	hand	(has)	(has)	her
pan	an	(pan)	pat	hand	(pan)	Pam

3. Write these words.

an   *an*

are   *are*

pan   *pan*

hand   *hand*

apple   *apple*

thank   *thank*

4. Read these sentences.

1. The man has a pan in his hand.
2. Cal looks at the girl's hands.
3. Dan and Ann are at Pam's shop.
4. Cal has a quarter for Dan.
5. Sam gives an apple to Van.

   Van thanks Sam.

6

Short Vowel Practices

If the student (S.) is using this workbook with *Laubach Way to Reading 2*, he should do the corresponding skill book lesson first. The directions and dialog for Practice 1-A that follow give you, the teacher or tutor (T.), a general pattern to follow for all the short vowel practices. You do not have to follow the dialog exactly, but make sure you are very familiar with it and with the suggestions for the teacher before you begin.

Before starting a practice, read any *Note* at the top of the practice page. A *Note* gives additional special directions *for that practice only*.

1

Part 1 gives words that will serve as key words to introduce word families. Many of these words have appeared in skill books 1 or 2. Those words that have *not* are starred (*). *Tell* the student these words.

T. says: You have learned that *i* has the short sound /i/.

Here are some words with the short *i* sound /i/.

What is this word? (Point to first word.) [S: Jill] Good.

And what is this word? (Point to next word.) [S: Hill] Good.

And this word? (Point to next word.) [S: Will] Good.

(If S. doesn't know the words, *tell* him the words: "This word is *Jill*. Read *Jill*.")

T. says: All of these words end with the letters *i-l-l*. (Point to *-ill*.)

The letter *i* has the short sound /i/ and *l* has the sound /l/.

So *i-l-l* sounds like /ill/.

You will learn some more words that end with *i-l-l*.

They sound like /ill/ at the end.

If there is more than one word family in the practice, go directly from this introduction to part 2 and have S. write the letters and read the words for the word family just introduced. Then return to part 1 again and introduce the next word family, following with part 2 for that word family. When S. has covered parts 1 and 2 for each word family, go on to part 3.

2 Write the letters and say the words.

T. says: What does *i-l-l* sound like? (Point to *ill* at the top of column.)

Practice 1-A: Word Family -ill

1.

Jill

Hill

Will

-ill

2. Write the letter or letters and say the word.

	ill			ill
b	_b_ ill	t	_t_ ill
f	_f_ ill	w	_w_ ill
h	_h_ ill	ch	_ch_ ill
k	_k_ ill	B	_B_ ill
m	_m_ ill	H	_H_ ill
p	_p_ ill	J	_J_ ill
		W	_W_ ill

3. Read the words.

pill	ill	Jill
mill	chill	Will
fill	kill	Hill
bill	till	Bill
will	hill	

4. Write the word you hear.

1. _kill_
2. _till_
3. _chill_
4. _mill_
5. _pill_
6. _hill_
7. _will_
8. _ill_
9. _fill_
10. _bill_
11. _Will_
12. _Bill_
13. _Jill_
14. _Hill_

[S: /ill/] Good. In fact, *i-l-l* is a word by itself, *ill*. It means *sick*. Read *ill*. [S: ill] Good.

You can make new words that sound like /ill/ at the end by putting one or two letters in front of *i-l-l*. What is this letter? (Point to *b*.) [S: b] Good. What sound does *b* make? [S: /b/] Good. Now write the letter *b* on the line in front of *i-l-l*. [S. does this.] What is this word? [S: bill] Good.

Help S. to make the other words. In exercises of this type, S. can make words using other consonants, digraphs, and consonant blends that he has learned. In this lesson, S. can use the digraph *ch*. In other lessons he can use *qu* and the digraphs *sh, th,* and *wh* to make words. He can also use consonant blends to make words, if those words occur in the skill book lesson (for instance, *truck, drop*). Point out that capital letters are used to begin names.

You probably won't have to follow such a detailed procedure with each word. Students who know the consonant sounds and who can blend sounds may automatically write down the letters and say the words. Some students may have great difficulty with this exercise, though.

As S. sounds out the words, you may want to talk about them. You may want to use the words in sentences or phrases that indicate their meanings. If there are several words in a practice whose meaning the student does not know, or if the student has difficulty learning so many words all at once, you may want to circle only the most common words for him to learn. (This is especially true for English-as-a-Second-Language students.) If you decide to omit some words in part 2, you should skip over them in parts 3 and 4 too.

The student may have to read through the words in part 2 more than once. When he can read most of them easily, he can go on to part 3. If it seems he needs much more practice with the words in part 2, you may want to stop work on the practice at this point and continue later, reviewing part 2 in the next teaching session.

3 Read the words.

T. says: Here are the same words that you have been making, in a new order.
Read the words.

If the student is learning only part of the word lists, skip over the words he is omitting. Check his reading. Help him only if he has any problems. If he has great difficulty with part 3, you should not go on with the practice. Give the student more exposure to those words later, perhaps in a different context.

In parts 3 and 4 of Practice 1-A, the names have been set apart from the other words. This is because there are several of them and because you want to point out that capital letters are used to begin names. In the following practices, names will not be set apart. The student should then know that the words are names if they begin with a capital letter. There are some common words that are names too, such as *bill, Bill; pat, Pat*. Those words are listed twice.

4 Write the word you hear.

T. says: Now I will read each of the words for you. Write the word you hear. (If the student is skipping some words in parts 2 and 3, skip them here too.)

Read the words slowly and distinctly. Repeat them as many times as necessary. The student may want to repeat a word after he hears it. If he misspells part of a word, read the word again, emphasizing the sound he missed. For example, if he writes *bill* for *fill*, you may say, "The beginning sound is different. *Fill. Fill.*" If he still has difficulty when you emphasize the sound, you may say, "The first sound is /f/. What letter makes the sound /f/?"

You may want to emphasize part 4 for students who are new readers or poor spellers. You can use part 4 as a basic spelling program where students can learn to spell many words easily. The student first spells words that are in the same word family, where only the beginning letters are different. If the practice has more than one family, the student writes all the words from one family together. He then writes the words from another family.

After the student has done a few of these practices, you may give him a sheet of paper and ask him to write down words from several word families mixed up together. Then he can review words he has trouble with.

Tell the student when the word is a name so he can use a capital letter. Check his capitalization. You may want to help him with his handwriting too.

12

5 Review Words, New Words, and Words from Skill Book 1

The words listed here will appear in the sentences in part 6.

Review Words are mostly from the corresponding skill book 2 lesson. A few are from an earlier lesson of skill book 2.

T. says: Here is a word you have read before. What is it? (If S. has read the word but doesn't remember it, refer back to the story it is in. If S. still has difficulty, tell him the word.)

If S. is not using *Laubach Way to Reading*, he may or may not know the words. If he does not, tell him the words.

T. says: Here are some other useful words to know. This word is _____ .

New Words are usually used at least three times in the sentences in part 6.

T. says: Here are some new words you will need in your reading. This word is _____ .

Go over the Review Words and the New Words, talking about what they mean, using them in sentences.

Point out things to help the student remember the words. Have him write these words. If S. has difficulty remembering or spelling a word, put it on a flashcard for him to review frequently. The student should know the words in part 5 fairly well before going on to part 6.

Words from skill book 1 that S. needs for reading part 6 are also listed. If S. has not read skill book 1, he should go over these words before going on to part 6. If you want to emphasize spelling or if you plan to have the student write the sentences, have him write these words too.

6 Read the sentences.

At this point the student has had practice reading and writing the word family words and some other basic vocabulary words. He should now be able to read meaningful sentences with those words in them.

Several of the words have more than one meaning so the sentences may suggest new meanings of words that you can discuss. You may need to explain some word or sentence meanings to the student if he seems confused. If he is skipping over some of the words in the word families, you should omit the sentences that have those words until such time as he has learned the words.

In some practices, not all the words in the word families are used in the sentences. This is because the words are less common, or because it is too difficult to make sentences with the words available.

---

5. Review Words

it   sister

Words from skill book 1

a	he	not
are	his	on
at	is	she
cup	Liz	snake
for	man	the
get	Mr.	this
has	Mrs.	up

6. Read the sentences.

1. Fill it up.
2. The mill is on the hill.
3. Will she get a chill?
4. This is Mr. Will Hill.
5. Is he ill?
6. This bill is for his sister.
7. Will the man kill the snake? He will not kill it.
8. Jill has a bill for the pills.
9. Liz is not his sister.
10. She will fill the cups.
11. Bill is up on the hill.
12. The pills are for his sister.
13. Chill it till 3.
14. Mrs. Hill has a sister.
15. Will he get a bill for it?
16. Bill is at the mill till 6.
17. Jill has a chill. She is ill.

7

Some students may read the sentences with great ease. For others the sentences will be a challenge.

As S. reads the sentences, note the following:

Does he see the connections between the words he has learned and the sentences he is now reading?

Does he recognize the most basic sight words easily? Does he need additional practice with some important words?

Does he know the word-family words well? Can he recognize them instantly, or must he sound them out? If he sounds out the words, can he do this well?

Does he confuse some words with some other similar words? What method does he use in decoding words? What words will he still need practice with?

Does he remember words from previous practices?

What are his skills and strengths in reading?

Does he understand the way words are used? Words that have several common meanings may often be used in more than one way. Occasionally words may be used as different parts of speech, such as *chill,* which is used as a noun and as a verb.

Does S. comprehend the whole sentence? Does he understand the different types of sentences–statements, commands, exclamations, questions? Does he notice the effect of punctuation? Does he read with expression?

S. may want to go over the sentences several times until he can read them easily. Any student who wants to improve his spelling and handwriting can also write the sentences as you dictate them. Because the sentences contain many words from previous practices, the student may want to first review the spellings of the sight words and the word families he has already had. When he can spell these words easily, he can go on to write the whole sentences. If S. still has trouble with some words when he writes them, you can have him write the words in a list or on cards to review.

If the student writes the sentences, call attention to the use of capital letters to begin the first word of every sentence and people's names.

Remember that there is no ideal amount of time recommended for these short vowel practices. One student may spend several days on one practice, and another may use it as a review and spend ten minutes on it. You must adapt the practices to the needs of your individual students.

Helping Students Decode Words Using a Word-Family Approach

A *word family* is a group of words that rhyme, where the ending stem is repeated with different beginning sounds. An example of a word family is this group of words: *pick, sick, lick, tick, kick, quick, chick,* and *thick.* The ending stem *-ick* is repeated with different beginning sounds.

The word-family approach used in the short vowel practices is a good way to help students learn new words.

When S. sees many words with the same ending stem, the sound-symbol relationships he is learning are reinforced. He can also generalize from a few words he knows to many words he does not know, so he can read and spell many words he has not had before.

Some students may have difficulties learning new words in families, however. If S. is doing the short vowel practices and has trouble with parts 2 or 3, note the area of difficulty and give specific help. For example:

1. If S. reads a word and gives the wrong beginning sound, have him identify the beginning letter or letters and the sounds they make. If S. makes many of these errors, he probably has an inadequate knowledge of consonant sounds, and he should review these sounds before continuing.

2. If S. gives the right beginning sound but mispronounces the ending stem, note the part of the stem which is missed (the vowel sound, the ending consonant sound, or both). Review the sounding of the stem, including the individual sounds and the blending of the sounds, and have S. repeat. Many errors of this type may indicate a problem with auditory memory, where S. has difficulty remembering sounds.

3. If S. mispronounces the entire word, review the sound of the stem, the beginning consonant sound, and the blending of the sounds into the word.

4. If S. cannot blend the sounds into words, go over the pronunciation of the sounds and the blending, having S. repeat. Try to pronounce the beginning consonant sounds without attaching a vowel sound (/b/—"buh") and to allow only a moment between pronouncing the beginning sound and the stem. You may also help S. practice blending by giving him beginning sounds and stems of words, a moment apart, having him blend the sounds into words.

Some students may struggle with blending sounds together, decoding words, or spelling words because they have not developed phonemic awareness skills. See Appendix A: Phonics, Phonemic Awareness, and the Process of Reading, for ideas to help these students.

Some students may find it very difficult to learn words by focusing on the ending stems. For these students, you may want to group words together that have similar beginnings instead of similar endings (e.g., *ran, ram, rat, rack*). Still other students may find it easier to learn words as wholes. They have difficulty learning words by breaking them down and sounding them out, or by blending sounds together. If you use a word-family approach with these students, you should avoid breaking words up into parts. For students who have difficulty learning with any of these approaches, you might want to try other techniques such as kinesthetic tracing.

Practice 1-B: Word Family -ick

1.   kick

   pick

   -ick

2. Write the letter or letters and say the word.

k _k_ ick   D _D_ ick

l _l_ ick   N _N_ ick

p _p_ ick   R _R_ ick

s _s_ ick

t _t_ ick

w _w_ ick

qu _qu_ ick

ch _ch_ ick

th _th_ ick

3. Read the words.

sick	lick	quick
tick	kick	Dick
wick	chick	pick
Nick	Rick	thick

4. Write the word you hear.

1. _pick_
2. _chick_
3. _tick_
4. _quick_
5. _sick_
6. _Dick_
7. _wick_
8. _kick_
9. _thick_
10. _Nick_
11. _lick_
12. _Rick_

5. Review Words

gift   big   little

New Words

me   we

Words from skill book 1

an	hand	pup
and	have	to
apple		

6. Read the sentences.

1. Nick is not sick.
2. We have a little chick.
3. Quick! Pick it up!
4. The pup will lick his hand.
5. Kick it to me.
6. It is not thick.
7. Will we get sick?
8. Dick picks up the bill for the gift.
9. It ticks and ticks.
10. The big pup licks the little pup.
11. Chill it till it gets thick.
12. Nick will pick an apple.
13. The pups have ticks.
14. The little chicks are quick.
15. Rick kicks me.
16. Pick a gift for me.
17. We have pills for the sick man.
18. Dick and Rick have a mill.

8

Practice 1-C: Word Families -ig, -iss, -is

1. big Miss his

　　-ig　　**-iss**　　**-is**

2. Write the letter or letters and say the word.

b *b* ig　　h *h* iss
d *d* ig　　k *k* iss
p *p* ig　　m *m* iss
w *w* ig　　M *M* iss

　　　　　　　　　is
　　　　　　h *h* is
　　　　　　th *th* is

3. Read the words.

wig　　　Miss
big　　　hiss
pig　　　kiss
dig　　　miss

his　　　this
　is

4. Write the word you hear.

1. *dig*
2. *big*
3. *wig*
4. *pig*
5. *kiss*
6. *miss*
7. *hiss*
8. *Miss*
9. *is*
10. *his*
11. *this*

5. Review Word

little

Words from skill book 1

girl　　give　　her　　I　　you

6. Read the sentences.

1. This is Miss Jill Hill.
2. This wig is thick.
3. Dig it up.
4. I miss you.
5. The snake will hiss.
6. It is little, not big.
7. He will kiss Miss Hill.
8. The pigs are not his.
9. Will you miss me?
10. Is this pig sick?
11. Will you kiss Jill's big sister?
12. Nick and I hiss at Bill.
13. This wig is big for you.
14. Rick digs on the hill.
15. I give her a big kiss.
16. Dick will miss his girl.
17. The pig is big, and the chick is little.
18. Bill gets a wig for his girl.

9

16

Practice 2-A: Word Family -it

1.   it

     sit

   -it

2. Write the letter or letters and say the word.

		it			l	_l_ it
b	_b_ it		p	_p_ it		
f	_f_ it		s	_s_ it		
h	_h_ it		w	_w_ it		
k	_k_ it		qu	_qu_ it		

3. Read the words.

kit	wit
sit	hit
it	pit
quit	bit
lit	fit

4. Write the word you hear.

1. _wit_
2. _pit_
3. _quit_
4. _fit_
5. _bit_
6. _sit_
7. _lit_
8. _it_
9. _kit_
10. _hit_

5. Review Word

with

New Word

your

Words from skill book 1

in	put	of	leg
dish	shop	olive	

6. Read the sentences.

1. I will dig a big pit.
2. She will quit.
3. Will the wig fit me?
4. Your pup bit the girl.
5. The shop is lit up.
6. Your sister sits with Rick.
7. Pick up this kit.
8. He has a quick wit.
9. Hit it with your hand.
10. The little pup bit his leg.
11. The sick man sits up.
12. It will not fit in the kit.
13. I will not quit till 6.
14. Put the olive pits in the dish.
15. It is little, and it will not fit me.
16. She is a girl with a wit.
17. He hits and kicks the man.
18. Give me a little bit of it.

10

Practice 2-B: Word Families -in, -im

1.   in   Kim

  -in   him

    -im

2. Write the letter or letters and say the word.

in

b _b_ in

f _f_ in   d _d_ im

p _p_ in   h _h_ im

s _s_ in   r _r_ im

t _t_ in   J _J_ im

w _w_ in   K _K_ im

ch _ch_ in   T _T_ im

sh _sh_ in

th _th_ in

3. Read the words.

tin	chin	Kim	dim
sin	win	him	Tim
in	thin	Jim	rim
shin	fin		
bin	pin		

4. Write the word you hear.

1. _win_   9. _tin_
2. _chin_   10. _fin_
3. _pin_   11. _Jim_
4. _sin_   12. _rim_
5. _thin_   13. _Kim_
6. _in_   14. _Tim_
7. _bin_   15. _him_
8. _shin_   16. _dim_

5. Review Word

dinner

New Word

into

Words from skill book 1

fish   quarter   they

6. Read the sentences.

1. A fish has fins.
2. I put a quarter into the man's tin cup.
3. Will they win it?
4. Jim and Tim have dinner.
   They have dinner with Kim.
5. I kick him in the shin.
6. Jim bit into an apple.
7. Kim is thin.
8. It is a sin to kill.
9. Jim has a big chin.
10. A pin is thin, not thick.
11. This is the rim of the cup.
12. They will not quit till they win.
13. It is dim in the mill.
14. The apples are in the bin.
15. Kim hit him on the chin.
16. Put the tin pins into this kit.
17. Tim gets a hit and wins.

11

Note: Point out the two words with consonant blends at the beginning, *bring* and *drink* (new word).

Practice 2-C: Word Families -ing, -ink

1.   sing   sink

      ring   rink

      -ing   **-ink**

2. Write the letter or letters and say the word.

k _k_ ing   ink
r _r_ ing   l _l_ ink
s _s_ ing   m _m_ ink
w _w_ ing   p _p_ ink
th _th_ ing   r _r_ ink
br _br_ ing s _s_ ink
            w _w_ ink
            th _th_ ink

3. Read the words.

ring	link
king	pink
thing	ink
sing	sink
bring	think
wing	wink
	mink
	rink

4. Write the word you hear.

1. wing   8. link
2. thing   9. ink
3. ring   10. pink
4. king   11. sink
5. bring   12. think
6. sing   13. rink
7. mink   14. wink

5. Review Word

finger

New Word

drink

Words from skill book 1

bird	neck
live	one
look	street
my	telephone

6. Read the sentences.

1. This ink is pink.
2. She puts the drink in the cups. He drinks one cup of it.
3. The bird has big wings.
4. I think Will lives on this street.
5. Give me a mink, not a ring.
6. Bring the things to the sink.
7. The birds sing.
8. I get ink on my fingers.
9. He has a ring on his finger.
10. Jim is at the rink with Jill.
11. They will sing for the king.
12. Bill winks at girls.
13. The telephone rings.
14. The pink cup is in the sink.
15. I think my ring will fit her finger.
16. Bring me a drink.
17. He gives things to my sister.

12

19

Note: Point out that the *wh* in *whip* has the same sound as in *whistle*. If S. pronounces *wh* and *w* the same way, don't worry about it.

Practice 2-D: Word Family -ip

1. lip

zip

-ip

2. Write the letter or letters and say the word.

d _d_ ip   t _t_ ip
h _h_ ip   z _z_ ip
l _l_ ip   wh _wh_ ip
n _n_ ip   sh _sh_ ip
r _r_ ip   ch _ch_ ip
s _s_ ip

3. Read the words.

nip   dip   ship
chip   sip   lip
zip   whip   hip
rip   tip

4. Write the word you hear.

1. _tip_
2. _rip_
3. _ship_
4. _nip_
5. _hip_
6. _chip_
7. _lip_
8. _whip_
9. _sip_
10. _dip_
11. _zip_

5. New Word

our

Words from skill book 1

zipper   hurt

6. Read the sentences.

1. Jim licks his lips.
2. She hurt her hip.
3. Dip it into the cup.
4. Kim rips up the bills.
5. This is the tip of the pin.
6. Dick has a big whip in his hand.
   He will not hit the pup with the whip.
7. Our ship will not sink.
8. Zip up the zipper.
9. Our pup nips at Bill's leg.
10. She fills the dish with chips.
11. She picks up the cup and sips the drink.
12. This will not fit at the hips.
13. Tim will kiss her on the lips.
14. The pup bit the tip of my finger.
15. The chip dip is in the pink dish.
16. She zips it up, and it rips.
17. Our sister is on the ship.

13

20

Practice 3-A: Word Families -id, -ib, -ix

1.   did   rib   six

    -id   -ib   -ix

2. Write the letter or letters and say the word.

b _b_ id   b _b_ ib
d _d_ id   r _r_ ib
h _h_ id
k _k_ id   f _f_ ix
l _l_ id   m _m_ ix
r _r_ id   s _s_ ix

3. Read the words.

rid   rib
hid   bib
lid
bid   mix
kid   six
did   fix

4. Write the word you hear.

1. _lid_   7. _rib_
2. _rid_   8. _bib_
3. _did_   9. _six_
4. _hid_   10. _mix_
5. _kid_   11. _fix_
6. _bid_

5. Review Words

city   Kitty   whistle

New Word

want

Words from skill book 1

two   pan

6. Read the sentences.

1. Mr. Hill has six kids.
2. Put the lid on the pan.
3. Get rid of the pills.
4. We hid her whistle.
5. Kitty did not mix up the bills.
6. I want you to fix the sink.
7. Bill hits Jim in the ribs.
8. Mrs. Hill puts a bib on her kid.
9. They bid on the things they want.
10. I think the two things will mix.
11. The kids did not live in the city.
12. My sister has six wigs.
13. Kitty will fix our dinner.
14. Bill and I want ribs for dinner.
15. The lid did not fit on the pan.
16. Nick wants to get rid of his things.
17. He did not want to bid on it.
18. The man hid in the city.

14

Note: Point out that the sound /ch/ is sometimes spelled
with a *c-h* and sometimes with *t-c-h*. Cover those
two families in a group, going from part 1 to part 2.

Practice 3-B: Word Families -ish, -ich, -itch, -ive

1.　　　dish　　　pitch

-ish　　**-itch**

　　　rich　　　give

-ich　　　live

　　　　　-ive

2. Write the letter or letters and say the word.

d _d_ ish　　　　　　itch
f _f_ ish　　　d _d_ itch
w _w_ ish　　　h _h_ itch
　　　　　　　p _p_ itch
r _r_ ich　　　w _w_ itch
wh _wh_ ich

　　　　　　　g _g_ ive
　　　　　　　l _l_ ive

3. Read the words.

dish　　rich　　hitch　　live
wish　　which　　itch　　give
fish　　　　pitch
　　　　　witch
　　　　　ditch

4. Write the word you hear.

1. _wish_　　7. _hitch_
2. _fish_　　8. _itch_
3. _dish_　　9. _witch_
4. _rich_　　10. _pitch_
5. _which_　11. _give_
6. _ditch_　12. _live_

5. Review Word

kitchen

New Words

be　　　　if

Word from skill book 1

river

6. Read the sentences.

1. Kim will fix fish in the kitchen.
2. He will hit and pitch.
3. They live on a ship on the river.
   Which river is it?
4. Did he dig this big ditch?
5. I will be rich if I get my wish.
6. This girl is not a witch.
7. I think he will be sick.
   If he gets sick, give him a pill.
8. My hands itch.
9. Our kids fish in the river.
10. Which dish is the chip dip in?
11. If you win it, you will be rich.
12. We wish we did not live in the city.
13. Give me a big dish for this fish.
14. Pitch it to me, and I will hit it.
15. Six kids hid in the ditch.
16. The rich man gives and gives.

15

22

Using the Endings Practices

In these practices, the student will learn when endings are used. He will learn how to add or take off endings on new words, and he will read and write many words with these endings. These practices can also be used by students not using the skill books who need remedial help.

Whenever possible, do these practices one-to-one with S., having S. read to you as he works along. In this way, you can hear S. pronounce the words and give him immediate help throughout the practices.

If any endings practice moves too rapidly or is otherwise too difficult for S., you may want to divide it up and work on only one skill at a time.

Many students will need more practice on endings than this workbook provides. Some students may not remember some words even after they have read them, studied them, and written them. For these students, you may want to make more worksheets, going over some of the same words and endings again.

Still other students remember the words they've studied, but they have trouble applying what they've learned about endings to new or different words. You can set up lessons to help your students apply what they've learned to other words.

Before doing any endings practice, S. should know the short vowel words from the previous word family practices fairly well. If S. occasionally has trouble with a root word, you may supply it. But if S. has trouble with many words, you should not continue the practice until S. is more familiar with the words.

Practice 3-C: Adding Endings

1 Adding -s to words to show that there is more than one

T. says: You have seen -s on the end of some words.

You can put -s on the end of words that name people, places, or things.

The -s means *more than one* person, place, or thing.

This says one shop. (Point to *one shop.*)

This says six shops. (Point to *six shops.*)

The -s on the end of *shops* shows that there is *more than one shop.*

Go over the other example, *girl.*

2 Add -s and read the word.

T. says: These are words that name people, places, or things. Read each word.

Then write the word and add -s to it. Read the word you have written.

What is this word? (Point to *hill.*) [S: hill]

Add -s to *hill,* like this. (Point to example.)

What is the word then? [S: hills] Good.

Do the other words. Make sure S. writes and pronounces them correctly.

3 Add -s to the word. Fill in the blank. Read the sentence.

T. says: Now look at this word in front of the sentence. (Point to *pig.*)

What is this word? [S: pig]

Write *pig* and add -s. [S. writes *pigs* on the blank.]

What is this word? [S: pigs] Good.

Now read the sentence. [S. reads the sentence.]

Continue with the other sentences. Some students may want to read the sentence first before writing in the word.

4 Adding -s to action words

T. says: You can also add -s to some action words when you are talking about *things that happen now.* You add -s when *he, she,* or *it* does something in the present time.

We say, "I sing" (point to first example), but "She sings." (Point.)

Jill is like *she,* so we say, "Jill sings." (Point.)

We say, "We kick," but "He kicks." (Point to example.)

Jim is like *he,* so we say, "Jim kicks." (Point.)

We say, "You sit," but "It sits." (Point to example.)

The pup is like *it,* so we say, "The pup sits." (Point.)

You may have to give students much more practice to develop the principle of adding -s to action words (verbs) in the present time with subjects like *he, she,* or *it.*

5   6

For parts 5 and 6, follow the same procedure as for parts 2 and 3.

7 Adding -ing to action words

T. says: You have seen *-ing* on the end of some action words.

With helping words like *is, am,* or *are,* you use *-ing* on the action word. With *is, am,* or are and *-ing* on the end of action words, you are talking about *things that are happening now.*

Read this word. (Point to *sing.*) [S: sing]

Read this sentence. (Point to *We are singing.*) [S: We are singing.] Good.

Follow the same procedure for the other two examples.

8   9

For parts 8 and 9, follow the same procedure as for parts 2 and 3, except with *-ing.*

Practice 3-C: Adding Endings

1. Adding *-s* to words to show that there is more than one

a	shop
six	shop<u>s</u>
one	girl
two	girl<u>s</u>

2. Add *-s* and read the word.

hill	_hills_
chick	_chicks_
lip	_lips_
thing	_things_
bill	_bills_
wig	_wigs_

3. Add *-s* to the word. Fill in the blank. Read the sentence.

1. pig   He sells ten _pigs_ .
2. ring   Jill has three _rings_ .
3. pin   Pick up the _pins_ .
4. kid   Kim has two _kids_ .
5. cup   I want six _cups_ .

4. Adding *-s* to action words

I	sing.
She	sing<u>s</u>.
Jill	sing<u>s</u>.
We	kick.
He	kick<u>s</u>.
Jim	kick<u>s</u>.
You	sit.
It	sit<u>s</u>.
The pup	sit<u>s</u>.

5. Add *-s* and read the word.

pick	_picks_
dig	_digs_
win	_wins_
live	_lives_
think	_thinks_
put	_puts_

6. Add *-s* to the word. Fill in the blank. Read the sentence.

1. bring   He _brings_ me gifts.
2. fill   She _fills_ up her cup.
3. lick   The pup _licks_ my hands.
4. wink   Bill _winks_ at Kim.
5. fit   The ring _fits_ Jim's finger.

7. Adding *-ing* to action words

sing	We are sing<u>ing</u>.
think	I am think<u>ing</u>.
fish	He is fish<u>ing</u>.

8. Add *-ing* and read the word.

fill	_filling_
mix	_mixing_
fish	_fishing_
bring	_bringing_
drink	_drinking_
pitch	_pitching_

9. Add *-ing* to the word. Fill in the blank. Read the sentence.

1. kiss   Tim is _kissing_ his girl.
2. sink   The ship is _sinking_ .
3. chill   Kim is _chilling_ the drink.
4. sing   Dick and Bill are _singing_ .
5. fix   Jill is _fixing_ the sink.

16

Practice 3-D: Review Lesson: Short *i*

In the review practices, S. reviews a number of words he has covered for a particular short vowel. Much of the work involves discriminating between beginning or ending consonants that look or sound alike.

All of the review practices are two pages. All follow the same format.

If the student makes eight or more errors on the whole review, he probably needs more help with consonant sounds, with short vowel sounds, or both. Note S's errors. If he confuses words, does he mistake words that *look* alike or *sound* alike? Do particular sounds or words give him trouble? Does he have more trouble with beginnings or endings of words?

He may need to be checked for vision or hearing problems.

1 Look at the picture and say the word. Then fill in the letter or letters to make the word.

T. says: Look at the picture and say the word.
Then fill in the right letter or letters to make the word.

Be sure S. says the correct word for the picture. S. then picks the letter or letters that make the beginning or ending sound that is missing. He picks one of two choices and writes the letter or letters in the blank. This is the easiest discrimination exercise.

T. says: What is this? (Point to picture.) [S: hill]
The beginning letter is missing.
What is the beginning sound in *hill*? [S: /h/]
Good.
What letter makes the sound /h/, *h* or *m*? (Point to letters.) [S: *h*]
Write the letter in the blank.

If you are not sure S. knows the two letters or their sounds, point to each letter and ask, "What is this letter? What sound does it make?" You may have the student pronounce the word made with the other letter, too:
"What sound would *m-i-l-l* be?"

2 Circle the word that makes sense in the sentence.

T. says: Look at the two words that are together in each sentence.
Read them.
Read the sentence with one word and again with the other word.
Circle the word that makes sense in the sentence.

Again S. picks from two words that have different beginning or ending sounds. He must read and understand the sentence and know the common meanings of the words in order to pick the right word.

3 Look at the picture and say the word. Then circle the right word.

T. says: Look at the picture and say the word. Then circle the right word.

Be sure S. says the correct word for the picture. You can have him read the choices before circling one. A few of the words may be new to the student, but he should be able to read them.

This part is like part 1 but is a little more difficult. There are *four* choices instead of two. S. must study whole words, not just beginnings or endings. The incorrect choices are words which have beginnings or endings like the correct word. The letter that is incorrect often looks like or sounds like the correct letter.

Practice 3-D: Review Lesson – Short i

1. Look at the picture and say the word. Then fill in the right letter to make the word.

 h
___ ill
m

 t
hi ___
p

 nk
si ___
ck

 d
___ ig
b

 r
___ id
l

 n
chi ___
p

2. Circle the word that makes sense in the sentence.

1. I lick / lit my lips.

2. Did Tim wing / wink at Jill?

3. I think I will fix bibs / ribs for dinner.

4. Mix up this dip for the chips / ships .

5. Mrs. Hill will kiss / kit the children.

6. If Dick sells his digs / pigs , he will be rich.

3. Look at the picture and say the word. Then circle the right word.

1.   rib   bib   did   bid

4.   bill   pill   till   hill

2.   lit   bit   hit   fit

5.   wick   wing   will   wink

3.   sip   sick   sit   six

6.   shin   ship   hip   chip

17

26

4 Look at the picture and say the word. Then write the word under the picture.

T. says: Look at the picture and say the word.

Then write the word under the picture.

This section is more difficult because S. must spell the whole word. Be sure he says the correct word for the picture.

5 Circle all the words that are the same as the first. Work from left to right.

T. says: Circle all the words that are the same as the first. Work from left to right.

This is primarily a *visual* discrimination exercise. It is useful for giving evidence of visual problems like poor vision, directional problems, and reversals of letters and words. Some of the incorrect words are new to the student, but they *look* like the word to be circled. In a few cases, an incorrect word is the same as the circled word except for the vowel. If the student makes an error by circling these words, he is probably not noticing the vowels in words. If the student makes many mistakes in this visual discrimination exercise (four or more), you should check for visual problems.

6 Read these sentences.

T. says: Read these sentences.

These sentences have words from all the different word families that S. has studied up to this point. S. should be able to read these fairly easily if he can read the sentences in the short vowel practices. Some students may want to practice their handwriting by copying these sentences.

27

4. Look at the picture and say the word. Then write the word under the picture.

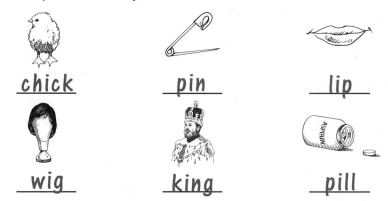

chick   pin   lip

wig   king   pill

5. Circle all the words that are the same as the first. Work from left to right.

pit	bit	pit	fit	pill	pit	tip	pit
bid	bid	big	did	bid	lid	hid	bid
hill	mill	lid	hill	bill	hill	kill	hit
fin	fix	fin	fin	fit	pin	fin	tin
nip	pin	whip	nip	hip	nip	pin	rip
lick	lick	kick	kill	live	lick	tick	lid
dig	big	dig	dip	dig	pig	big	did
ring	ring	rim	rink	ring	bring	rig	ring

6. Read these sentences.

1. Kim will fill up six cups with the drink.

2. Bill picks up the big dish and brings it to the sink.

3. His finger is thin, and the ring will not fit on it.

4. If Jim hits and you pitch, we will win!

5. I wish you did not have to quit. We will miss you.

6. If Mr. King gets sick with a chill, give him this pill.

7. Which city did Rick live in?

8. Whip the mix till it gets thick.

18

Practice 4-A: Word Families -un, -um

1.   r u n   g u m

  g u n   **-um**

  s u n

  -un

2. Write the letter or letters and say the word.

b _*b*_ un   b _*b*_ um

f _*f*_ un   g _*g*_ um

g _*g*_ un   h _*h*_ um

n _*n*_ un   r _*r*_ um

r _*r*_ un   s _*s*_ um

s _*s*_ un

3. Read the words.

nun   gum

sun   rum

gun   bum

run   hum

bun   sum

fun

4. Write the word you hear.

1. _*run*_   7. _*hum*_

2. _*gun*_   8. _*rum*_

3. _*sun*_   9. _*gum*_

4. _*fun*_   10. _*sum*_

5. _*nun*_   11. _*bum*_

6. _*bun*_

5. Review Words

son   hunt

New Word

out

Words from skill book 1

Ann   children   do   sell

6. Read the sentences.

1. Kim will sing, and I will hum.
2. He puts the fish on a bun.
3. My son thinks it is fun to hunt.
   He is out hunting with his gun.
4. The man is a bum.
5. Do they sell gum in this shop?
6. Sister Ann is a nun.
7. The sum of 2 and 4 is 6.
8. Run and get my gun.
9. He has a drink of rum.
10. Is the sun up?
11. The nun hums and sings.
12. The children have fun out in the sun.
13. Do not run with a gun in your hand.
14. Sum it up for me.
15. My son puts the buns in the dish.
16. He wants me to give him gum.
    I do not have gum. I have run out of it.

19

Note: Point out that the sound /us/ is sometimes spelled
     with u-s and sometimes with u-s-s. Cover those two
     families as a group in going from part 1 to part 2.

Practice 4-B: Word Families -up, -ub, -us, -uss

1.   cup   rub   bus   fuss
     pup   **-ub**   **-us**   **-uss**
     -up

2. Write the letter or letters and say the word.

        up   us
    c _c_ up   b _b_ us
    p _p_ up   th _th_ us

    c _c_ ub   c _c_ uss
    r _r_ ub   f _f_ uss
    t _t_ ub

3. Read the words.

    up   rub   bus   fuss
    cup   tub   us   cuss
    pup   cub   thus

4. Write the word you hear.

    1. _pup_   7. _us_
    2. _up_   8. _bus_
    3. _cup_   9. _thus_
    4. _tub_   10. _fuss_
    5. _rub_   11. _cuss_
    6. _cub_

5. **Review Words**

    son   hunt

    New Words

    husband   just

    Words from skill book 1

    go   jump   tell   under   woman

6. Read the sentences.

    1. The woman fills up the tub.
    2. He rubs the pup's neck.
    3. My husband is picking up our pup.
    4. Put the cups in the sink.
    5. Just six of us will go on this bus.
       He will just miss his bus.
    6. The woman rubs her hands.
    7. Do not cuss at us!
    8. The little cubs jump and run.
    9. The kids will fuss if they do not go
       with us.
    10. The pups run under the bus.
    11. My husband is sick. Thus, he will not
        go with us.
    12. The woman has just two cups.
    13. My husband runs up the street to get
        the bus.
    14. The woman sits in the tub.
    15. If your leg hurts, rub it.
    16. The woman tells her husband, "Do not
        fuss at me."
    17. Did the Cubs win?

20

Practice 4-C: Word Families -ut, -ud, -uff

1. cut   mud   puff

    -ut   **-ud**   **-uff**

2. Write the letter or letters and say the word.

b *b* ut   b *b* ud

c *c* ut   m *m* ud

h *h* ut   B *B* ud

r *r* ut

n *n* ut   c *c* uff

sh *sh* ut   m *m* uff

             p *p* uff

3. Read the words.

hut	Bud	puff
rut	mud	muff
nut	bud	cuff
but		
shut		
cut		

4. Write the word you hear.

1. *nut*   7. *bud*
2. *shut*   8. *Bud*
3. *cut*   9. *mud*
4. *rut*   10. *muff*
5. *but*   11. *puff*
6. *hut*   12. *cuff*

5. Review Words

duck   hunt   Jimmy

Words from skill book 1

box   no

6. Read the sentences.

1. Cut up the duck for us.
2. Jimmy gets mud on his cuff.
3. She shut up the shop.
4. Kitty is looking at the little pink buds.
   The buds are little, but they will get big.
5. Bill has no cuts on his hands.
6. The man lives in a hut.
   The hut has mud on it.
7. The woman gives nuts and gum to the kids.
8. I want to hunt ducks, but I have no gun.
9. Bud will not shut the box.
10. She puts her hands into the muff.
11. He gets a cut on his lip.
    His lip will puff up and get big.
12. The bus is in a big rut, but we will get it out.
13. We had fun hunting for nuts.
14. The woman tells the kids to shut up.
15. No one but Jill gets cut.

21

Practice 4-D: Word Families -ug, -udge

1. rug   judge

    jug   **-udge**

    -ug

2. Write the letter or letters and say the word.

b _b_ ug   b _b_ udge
d _d_ ug   f _f_ udge
h _h_ ug   j _j_ udge
j _j_ ug   n _n_ udge
m _m_ ug
r _r_ ug
t _t_ ug

3. Read the words.

hug   fudge

tug   nudge

mug   budge

bug   judge

jug

dug

rug

4. Write the word you hear.

1. _jug_   7. _bug_
2. _rug_   8. _judge_
3. _mug_   9. _fudge_
4. _dug_   10. _nudge_
5. _tug_   11. _budge_
6. _hug_

5. New Word

water

6. Read the sentences.

1. The woman hugs her son.
2. The jug has rum in it.
3. Is he a judge?
4. He tugs on the big rug.
5. The pup dug in the mud.
6. Put the water in a mug, not in a cup.
   Fill the mug with water.
7. I give Bud a nudge.
8. A big bug is under the rug.
9. Bill gives Kim a box of fudge.
   The fudge has nuts in it.
10. I hug and kiss my husband.
11. He will judge the pigs.
12. My son tugs on my hand.
13. I tug on the box, but it will not budge.
14. This cup of water has a bug in it.
15. Her pup gets mud on the rug.
16. He drinks out of the water jug.

22

Practice 5-A: Word Families -uck, -ush, -uch

1.   duck   rush   much

    Buck   **-ush**   **-uch**

    -uck

2. Write the letter or letters and say the word.

b	*b* uck	g	*g* ush	
d	*d* uck	h	*h* ush	
l	*l* uck	r	*r* ush	
s	*s* uck	m	*m* ush	
t	*t* uck			
st	*st* uck	m	*m* uch	
tr	*tr* uck	s	*s* uch	
B	*B* uck			
Ch	*Ch* uck			

3. Read the words.

tuck	duck	mush	such
luck	suck	hush	much
buck	truck	gush	
stuck	Buck	rush	
Chuck			

4. Write the word you hear.

1.	*Buck*	9.	*buck*
2.	*suck*	10.	*rush*
3.	*duck*	11.	*mush*
4.	*tuck*	12.	*hush*
5.	*truck*	13.	*gush*
6.	*Chuck*	14.	*such*
7.	*stuck*	15.	*much*
8.	*luck*		

5. **Review Words**

does   from   come   some

New Words

so   good

Words from skill book 1

thank   visit

6. Read the sentences.

1. Bud Buck comes from the city in his truck.

   Does his truck get stuck in the mud?

2. Kitty is fixing me some ducks for dinner.

   I tell her, "Thanks so much for such a good dinner."

3. Tuck it in.

4. Bud has such good luck.

5. He sells us some apples for two bucks.

6. Do not rush so much!

7. It is so good to have Chuck come to visit us.

8. Sam and Jim rush out of the shop.

9. Do not put so much mush in my dish.

   I just want a little.

10. The gum gets stuck on my fingers.

11. Mrs. Buck tells her children to hush.

12. He does not have good luck fixing trucks.

13. The fudge is stuck to the pan.

14. The little girl sucks on her finger.

15. Chuck has good luck hunting. He gets a big buck.

23

Practice 5-B: Word Families -ung, -unk

1.　sung　　sunk

　　-ung　　junk

　　　　　-unk

2. Write the letter or letters and say the word.

h _h_ ung　　b _b_ unk
l _l_ ung　　d _d_ unk
r _r_ ung　　h _h_ unk
s _s_ ung　　j _j_ unk
　　　　　p _p_ unk
　　　　　s _s_ unk
　　　　　ch _ch_ unk

3. Read the words.

rung　　junk　　chunk
hung　　sunk　　dunk
sung　　hunk　　punk
lung　　bunk

4. Write the word you hear.

1. _sung_　　7. _sunk_
2. _rung_　　8. _dunk_
3. _lung_　　9. _hunk_
4. _hung_　　10. _bunk_
5. _punk_　　11. _junk_
6. _chunk_

5. Review Words

funny　　mother　　brother
uncle　　picture　　word

New Words

other　　like

6. Read the sentences.

1. My brother likes to sit on his bunk.
2. Uncle Bud will get rid of the junk.
3. Dunk it under the water.
4. Mother hung up one other picture.
5. My brother Chuck has sung for us.
   We like the funny words he has sung.
6. A fish has no lungs.
7. Bill likes to dunk his sister in the water.
   The little punk thinks it is funny!
8. This hunk of tin is no good to us.
   Put it with the other junk.
9. The ship has sunk under the water.
10. Mother cuts a big chunk of fudge.
11. The picture from my uncle looks like junk to us.
    It looks funny, so we have not hung it up.
12. The telephone has rung. Did she get it?
    She did pick it up, but they hung up.
13. I want this bunk, not the other one.

24

Practice 5-C: Adding Endings (CVC + C + *ing*)

1 Adding *-ing* to VCC Words

T. says: Look at *hunt. Hunt* ends with a Vowel-Consonant-Consonant. (Point to VCC label.)

To write *hunting,* just add *-ing.* (Point to *hunting.*)

When a word ends with Vowel-Consonant-Consonant, just add *-ing.*

Go over the other examples with the student.

2 Label the last three letters. Write the word with *-ing.*

T. says: Look at *jump.* (Point to *jump.*) Label the last three letters.

Write *V* for "vowel" and *C* for "consonant."
[S. labels them VCC.]

Now write *jumping.* [S. writes the word.] Good.

Do the rest of the words the same way.

3 Add *-ing* to the word. Read the sentences.

T. says: Look at the word in front of the sentence.
Write it in the blank. Add *-ing* to the word.
Read the sentence.

4 Adding *-ing* to CVC words

T. says: Look at *run.*

It ends with a Consonant-Vowel-Consonant. (Point to CVC label.)

To write *running,* you must double the last letter *n* before adding *-ing.*

When a word ends with Consonant-Vowel-Consonant, you must double the last consonant (point to + C) before adding *-ing.* (Point to *-ing.*)

Go over the other examples with S.

5 Label the last three letters. Write the word with *-ing.*

T. says: Now look at *hug.* (Point to *hug.*) Label the last three letters.
[S. labels them CVC.]
Now write *hugging.* [S. writes the word.] Good.

Do the rest of the words the same way.

6 Add *-ing* to the word. Read the sentences.

Follow the same procedure as for part 3.

7 Label the last three letters with VCC or CVC. Write the word with *-ing.* Read the word.

T. says: Label the last three letters of each word with VCC or CVC.

Then write the word with the ending *-ing* and read it.

8 Take off the *-ing.* Write the root word. For some words you may have to take off a letter.

T. says: Now you will take the ending *-ing* off of words to find the root word.

The *root word* is the word before you add any endings.

For example, *jump* is the root word of *jumping* and *pick* is the root word of *picks.*

What is this word? (Point to *ripping.*) [S: ripping]

What is the *root word* of *ripping*? [S: rip] Good.

Write *rip* in the blank. (If S. writes *ripp,* say, "Remember the words in the *i-p* family? We spell *rip r-i-p.* Why are there two *p*'s in *ripping* then?" If S. doesn't know, say, "Because *rip* ends with a Consonant-Vowel-Consonant, so you have to double the last letter *p* before adding *-ing.*")

Now you do the next three words. (Then check S.'s work. Be sure he understands the rule and spells root words correctly.)

What is this word? (Point to *fussing.*) [S: fussing]

What is the *root word* of *fussing*? [S: fuss] Good.

Write *fuss* in the blank.

In *fuss,* both *s*'s are part of the root word.

Many root words end with double *s* or double *l* or double *f.*

Notes: 1. The CVC + C + *ing* rule applies only to one-syllable and two- syllable words with the stress on the last syllable. Compare *ad mit', admitting,* with *vis' it, visiting.*

          2. With words that end with *w* or *x,* do not double the last letter: *snows, snowing; mix, mixing.*

          3. With *qu* words, think of *qu* together as a consonant: *quit, quitting.*

          4. With VVC words, just add *-ing: look, looking.*

          5. Some words have three consonants at the end. They would be labeled *VCCC.* Just as with *VCC,* you can just add *-ing,* as with *catch, catching.*

35

Practice 5-C: Adding Endings

1. Adding *-ing* to VCC words

VCC + i n g

h u n t + i n g ⟶ hunting

f i l l + i n g ⟶ filling

t h i n k + i n g ⟶ thinking

2. Label the last three letters. Write the word with *-ing*.

VCC
jump *jumping*

VCC
kiss *kissing*

VCC
fish *fishing*

VCC
bring *bringing*

3. Add *-ing* to the word. Read the sentence.

drink 1. Are you _*drinking*_ this?

hurt 2. Bud's leg is _*hurting*_ him.

dunk 3. He is _*dunking*_ it in water.

4. Adding *-ing* to CVC words

C V C + C + i n g

r u n + n + i n g ⟶ running

s h i p + p + i n g ⟶ shipping

h u m + m + i n g ⟶ humming

5. Label the last three letters. Write the word with *-ing*.

CVC
hug *hugging*

CVC
bid *bidding*

CVC
dig *digging*

CVC
dip *dipping*

6. Add *-ing* to the word. Read the sentence.

hug 1. Mother is _*hugging*_ her kids.

shut 2. She is _*shutting*_ up the shop.

run 3. Dick is _*running*_ up the hill.

7. Label the last three letters with VCC or CVC. Write the word with *-ing*. Read the word.

VCC
rush *rushing*

CVC
bud *budding*

CVC
get *getting*

VCC
pick *picking*

VCC
lick *licking*

VCC
want *wanting*

VCC
chill *chilling*

CVC
cut *cutting*

VCC
fill *filling*

CVC
rub *rubbing*

VCC
rush *rushing*

CVC
tip *tipping*

8. Take off the *-ing*. Write the root word. For some words you may have to take off a letter.

ripping *rip*

pinning *pin*

shutting *shut*

fussing *fuss*

wishing *wish*

Practice 5-D: Contrasting Short Vowels: *i* and *u*

Many students have difficulty identifying the short vowel sounds in words. They often confuse one vowel sound with another. These contrasting short vowel exercises give the student much more practice with short vowel sounds. The student learns to tell similar vowel sounds apart, and how to read and spell words with particular vowel sounds.

The practices contrast only *two* vowels at a time, to avoid confusing the student with many vowel sounds.

If you think S. may already know the vowel sounds, give him the following pretest. If he completes it with no errors, you can assume he knows the short vowel sounds in the middle of words, and you could skip the contrasting short vowel practices.

Pretest:

Write the five vowels at the top of a page. Ask the student to number from 1–40. Tell him you will read some words and you want him to listen for the vowel sound in the word. Tell him you want him to write the short vowel that makes the sound for that word. Sometimes the vowel is at the beginning of a word. Sometimes it is in the middle. Note if the student has more trouble with one kind of word or the other.

tuck	hot	us	in	rash	fed	lid	pit
when	tan	less	dock	let	job	fell	leg
rib	fish	hip	beg	rut	ditch	puff	loss
mass	pod	lab	up	wag	chat	spot	tub
nun	check	mop	ink	gum	rug	tank	patch

For the student who does not know the vowel sounds and who does all the contrasting practices, you could use the above for a posttest at the end of this book. You can make up similar tests and exercises using words from the word families that the student has studied up to that point.

Dialog for Practice 5-D

In the dialog, slash marks around a vowel stand for the *short sound* of the vowel. This dialog can be followed in the other Contrasting Short Vowels exercises just by changing the vowels.

T. says: You have studied the short vowels *i* and *u*.
(Point to the letters at the top.)
This practice will help you tell the sounds apart.
What is the short sound of *i*? [S: /i/]
And the short sound of *u*? [S: /u/] Good.
Now I will read some pairs of words.
They are just alike except for the vowels.
The first word has the short *i* sound /i/.
The second word has the short *u* sound /u/.

T. says: You read the words after me. Notice the different sounds with the different vowels.
Rib. [S: rib] *Rub.* [S: rub]
Did you notice that the words sound different because the vowels are different?

Encourage S. to sound out the other pairs of words himself if he can.

1 Write the letter.

T. says: Here are some more pairs of words.
They are just alike except that the first word has *i* and the second one has *u*.
You read the two words, then look at the picture in the box.
One of the words names the picture.
You write the correct vowel, *i* or *u*, in the blank, to spell the name of the picture.

Be sure S. pronounces the words correctly and writes in the correct vowel. If S. makes an error, you can correct it right after he makes it, or at the end of part 1.

2 Circle the word that you hear.

T. says: Here are some more pairs of words like those you read.
I will read one word from each pair.
You listen to the vowel sound.
If you hear the short *i* sound /i/, circle the first word.
If you hear the short *u* sound /u/, circle the second word.

Read each word at least twice, slowly and distinctly. At the end of part 2, go back over any words that S. has missed and correct them.

3 Write the short vowel that you hear.

T. says: Now I will read some words.
You listen to the vowel sound.
If you hear the short *i* sound /i/, write *i* in the blank
If you hear the short *u* sound /u/, write *u* in the blank.

4 Circle the right word.

T. says: Look at the two words that are together in each sentence, and read them.
Read the sentence with one word and again with the other word.
Circle the word that makes sense in the sentence.

S. must read the words and understand the sentence to pick the right word.

Practice 5-D: Contrasting Short Vowels i and u

i	rib	dig	lick	bid	him	sing
u	rub	dug	luck	bud	hum	sung

1. Write the letter.

1. fin
   fun
   f _i_ n

3. sin
   sun
   s _u_ n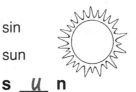

5. sink
   sunk
   s _i_ nk

2. rig
   rug
   r _u_ g

4. hit
   hut
   h _u_ t

2. Circle the word that you hear.

1. big (bug)
2. (lick) luck
3. (rib) rub

4. miss (muss)
5. (bin) bun
6. him (hum)

7. (bit) but
8. (chick) chuck
9. (rim) rum

10. hitch (hutch)
11. (dig) dug
12. sick (suck)

13. this (thus)
14. (pin) pun
15. ring (rung)

3. Write the short vowel that you hear.

1. t _u_ ck
2. s _i_ p
3. th _i_ nk

4. m _u_ ff
5. p _i_ g
6. b _i_ d

7. s _i_ ng
8. j _u_ g
9. h _u_ nk

10. f _u_ zz
11. p _i_ t
12. r _u_ t

13. c _u_ d
14. ch _i_ n
15. s _u_ ch

4. Circle the right word.

1. She will ___ her hands.
   rib
   (rub)

2. Bring me the ___ dish.
   (pink)
   punk

3. The pup ___ my leg.
   (bit)
   but

4. We wish him good ___.
   lick
   (luck)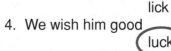

5. I sing and ___ to the children.
   him
   (hum)

6. The ___ is on her finger.
   (ring)
   rung

26

38

Practice 5-E: Review Lesson - Short u

1. Look at the picture and say the word. Then fill in the right letter to make the word.

h
_h_ ug
r

n
bu _n_
m

n
pu _p_ ff
p

t
cu _t_
b

l
_l_ uck
p

f
_j_ udge
j

2. Circle the word that makes sense in the sentence.

1. A bug bit his hand. Did his hand ____ up?
puck
(puff)

2. Do not ____ the mud on the rug.
(rub)
cub

3. Bud put the box under his ____.
buck
(bunk)

4. The ____ is stuck on my hands.
hum
(gum)
sung

5. Has she ____ for us?
(sung)
sunk

6. The bum is drinking some ____.
(rum)
run

3. Look at the picture and say the word. Then circle the right word.

1. (mug)   hug   jug   rug

4. buzz   (bus)   buck   but

2. puff   cut   (cuff)   cuss

5. cub   up   cut   (cup)

3. sung   (sun)   sum   sunk

6. nut   run   (nun)   fun

27

39

Practice 5-E: Review Lesson - Short u (continued)

4. Look at the picture and say the word. Then write the word under the picture.

tub   gum   nut

jug   duck   run

5. Circle all the words that are the same as the first. Work from left to right.

tug	lug	(tug)	tub	gut	(tug)	hug	(tug)
bud	(bud)	but	dub	(bud)	dud	bid	bug
cut	tuck	out	(cut)	cub	rut	put	(cut)
gum	gun	hum	(gum)	bum	mug	(gum)	gun
luck	(luck)	lung	lick	tuck	(luck)	look	buck
run	sun	nun	(run)	rum	(run)	rung	(run)
bus	bun	(bus)	sub	pus	(bus)	us	sub
pup	pub	(pup)	cup	dud	pug	(pup)	puff

6. Read these sentences.

   1. Mrs. Buck puts one cup of nuts in the fudge.

   2. Chuck's bus is stuck in a big rut.

       But my uncle will get it out with the truck.

   3. The kids fuss until Mother says, "Hush!"

   4. I hung up a picture of my uncle. He is a judge.

   5. This rug is not much good. Put it out with the junk.

   6. We had such fun hunting and fishing.

   7. I rush up to my son and hug him.

28

Practice 6-A: Word Family -ell

1. yell
    sell
    well
    -ell

2. Write the letter or letters and say the word.

b _b_ ell   w _w_ ell
f _f_ ell   y _y_ ell
h _h_ ell   sh _sh_ ell
s _s_ ell   B _B_ ell
t _t_ ell   N _N_ ell

3. Read the words.

well   Bell
bell   shell
sell   Nell
hell   fell
tell   yell

4. Write the word you hear.

1. _fell_   6. _well_
2. _sell_   7. _Nell_
3. _yell_   8. _hell_
4. _bell_   9. _Bell_
5. _shell_   10. _tell_

5. **Review Words**

help   twelve   very   fresh   many

New Words

until   jelly

Words from skill book 1

egg   seven

6. Read the sentences.

1. The woman tells us she has twelve children.
2. Mr. Bell has many fresh eggs to sell.
   He sells us a box of twelve fresh eggs.
3. I will help the sick man until he gets well.
4. Bud yells to Mr. Bell, "Help! Help!"
5. She fell and hurt her leg.
6. We will not have dinner until seven.
7. Nell picks up many shells from the water.
8. The woman sings very well.
9. The bell will ring at twelve.
10. He does not want to go to hell.
11. She yells, but no one comes to help.
12. Get the nut out of the shell.
13. Nell sells very good jelly at her shop.
    Bud tells us to get some apple jelly from her.
14. The little girl fell into a big well.
15. Tell your brother not to yell at me.
16. The children yell until the bell rings.

29

Practice 6-B: Word Family -et

1. get

pet

-et

2. Write the letter or letters and say the word.

b _b_ et   p _p_ et
g _g_ et   s _s_ et
j _j_ et   v _v_ et
l _l_ et   w _w_ et
m _m_ et   y _y_ et
n _n_ et

3. Read the words.

set   get   bet

pet   vet   met

net   let   jet

yet   wet

4. Write the word you hear.

1. _wet_   7. _met_
2. _let_   8. _yet_
3. _bet_   9. _jet_
4. _set_   10. _gte_
5. _pet_   11. _net_
6. _vet_

5. Review Words

cents   seventy

New Words

any   must   there   TV

Words from skill book 1

says   yes

6. Read the sentences.

1. Jimmy says a pup is a very good pet.
2. Mr. Bell will get on a big jet.
3. Set the eggs there.
4. Have you met my brother yet?
5. Mother will not let the kids look at TV.
6. Are there any fish in the net?
7. He must rush his pet to the vet.
   The vet will set the pup's leg.
8. Bill will bet seventy cents.
9. Yes, he met her there for dinner.
10. I must sell my TV set.
11. The pup jumps into the tub and gets wet.
12. He does not let the children have any pets.
13. You must fix the net if you want to get any fish.
14. I bet he will not get there until twelve.
15. The sun has not set yet.
16. Yes, let us go there on a jet.
17. I do not want to bet.

30

Practice 6-C: Word Families -en, -eck

1.   hen   neck

ten   **-eck**

men

-en

2. Write the letter or letters and say the word.

d _d_ en   th _th_ en   d _d_ eck

h _h_ en   wh _wh_ en   n _n_ eck

m _m_ en   B _B_ en   p _p_ eck

p _p_ en   K _K_ en   ch _ch_ eck

t _t_ en

3. Read the words.

men	pen	peck
ten	then	neck
Ben	Ken	check
hen	when	deck
den		

4. Write the word you hear.

1. _Ben_
2. _pen_
3. _when_
4. _ten_
5. _Ken_
6. _hen_
7. _men_
8. _den_
9. _then_
10. _neck_
11. _deck_
12. _check_
13. _peck_

5. Review Words

cents   twelve

New Word

women

Words from skill book 1

four   Glenn   Pam   tent   write

6. Read the sentences.

1. The deck of the ship is wet.
2. Pam is a woman. Pam and Ann are women.

   Ken is a man. Ken and Ben are men.
3. Glenn writes a check for the TV set.
4. Ken is sitting in his den with two men.
5. This pen is just ten cents, but it writes well.
6. If the bus does not run, then the men will check it.
7. The chick pecks at the egg to get out of it.

   The little chick will get to be a big hen.
8. When Ben is four, then Ken will be ten.
9. When will the dinner be? At seven.

   Twelve men and ten women are coming then.
10. Ben's neck hurts.
11. The little cubs live in the den.
12. The women write checks when they shop.
13. Ten big hens are in the pen.
14. Does the tent have a rip? Check it.
15. Men and women are sitting on the deck.

31

Note: Point out *egg,* spelled with two *g's* instead of one, and *guess,* spelled with a *u.* Also, *yes,* used in the sentences, is spelled with only one *s.*

Practice 7-A: Word Families -eg, -ess

1.　　leg　　less

　　　-eg　　　-ess

2. Write the letter or letters and say the word.

	egg	gu	_gu_ ess
b	_b_ eg	l	_l_ ess
k	_k_ eg	m	_m_ ess
l	_l_ eg	ch	_ch_ ess
p	_p_ eg	B	_B_ ess
M	_M_ eg	J	_J_ ess
P	_P_ eg		

3. Read the words.

peg	beg	guess
leg	Meg	less
egg		Jess
keg	mess	chess
Peg	Bess	

4. Write the word you hear.

1. _keg_   8. _less_
2. _egg_   9. _Bess_
3. _Meg_   10. _chess_
4. _peg_   11. _Jess_
5. _beg_   12. _mess_
6. _leg_   13. _guess_
7. _Peg_

5. **Review Words**

quickly　　pretty　　　them

New Words

best　　dress　　make　　unless

Words from skill book 1

address　　nest　　valley

6. Read the sentences.

1. Meg will get the best dress at the shop.

   The dress is selling for much less.

2. Peg gives a chess set to them.

3. He will run unless his leg hurts.

4. You must have the pegs to put up the tent.

5. Jess is bringing a keg of rum.

6. I will have to guess unless you tell me.

7. Bess begs the kids not to make a mess.

8. Yes, I guess this box of eggs is the best.

9. Write your address on the check.

10. It is less windy in the valley.

11. Mother tells them to pick up the mess quickly.

12. Jess will get some eggs from the hens' nests.

13. Did Ken make the best guess?

14. I will not win at chess unless you help me.

15. Your dress makes you look very pretty.

16. The man begs them for a quarter.

17. Peg makes a mess in the kitchen.

32

Practice 7-B: Word Families -ed, -edge

1.
Ed	edge
bed	ledge
red	**-edge**
-ed	

2. Write the letter or letters and say the word.

b	_b_ ed			Ed			edge
f	_f_ ed	Fr	_Fr_ ed	h	_h_ edge
l	_l_ ed	N	_N_ ed	l	_l_ edge
r	_r_ ed	T	_T_ ed	w	_w_ edge
w	_w_ ed						
sh	_sh_ ed						

3. Read the words.

led	red	hedge
wed	Ted	edge
shed	Ned	wedge
Ed	fed	ledge
bed	Fred	

4. Write the word you hear.

1. _fed_
2. _red_
3. _Ted_
4. _wed_
5. _Ned_
6. _led_
7. _bed_
8. _shed_
9. _Fred_
10. _Ed_
11. _ledge_
12. _wedge_
13. _edge_
14. _hedge_

5. Review Words

send   friend   letter

New Words

sent   went   wedding

6. Read the sentences.

1. Did Ed send letters to any of his friends?

   Yes, he sent a letter to his friend Ted.

2. Ned went out to the shed to get a pick.

3. Fred will cut the hedge for me.

4. Mother fed her children and sent them to bed.

   They went to bed at ten.

5. Meg wants a pretty wedding.

6. Ted went to the city in his red truck.

7. The bird makes a nest on the ledge.

8. Ned and Ted fed the pets.

9. He led them to the edge of the river.

10. Does your pup shed?

11. Bess sent Meg a pretty red dress.

12. When will Ned and Peg be wed?

    I want to go to the wedding and send a gift.

13. Fred sits on the edge of his bed.

14. Ed's neck gets red when he sits in the sun.

15. This wedge has a thin edge.

33

45

Practice 7-C: Adding Endings

1. To add *-ing* to a word that ends with *-e*, take off the *-e* and add *-ing*.

g i v e̸ + i n g → giving

n u d g e̸ + i n g → nudging

m a k e̸ + i n g → making

2. Add *-ing* and read the word.

live	living
have	having
come	coming
whistle	whistling
judge	judging
like	liking

3. Take off the *-e*, and add *-ing* to the word under the blank. Read the sentences.

1. Bess is **writing** letters.
   write
2. Ed is **judging** the pigs.
   judge
3. We are **making** apple jelly.
   make

4. Reviewing endings
Take off the *-s* ending, and read the word.

whips	whip
sets	set
makes	make
puffs	puff
quits	quit
says	say
brings	bring
tells	tell
ticks	tick

5. Reviewing endings
Add *-ing* to the word and fill in the blank. (For some words you may have to take off the *-e*. For some words you will have to double the last letter.) Read the sentences.

1. send — They are **sending** you a check.
2. bet — Fred is **betting** seventy cents.
3. dress — Peg is **dressing** her little kids.
4. come — Dick is **coming** to dinner.
5. whistle — Ted is **whistling** for the pup.
6. let — She is **letting** us go to the city.
7. check — The men are **checking** the truck.
8. rush — Jimmy is **rushing** to the shop.
9. take — The kids are **taking** the cups to the sink.

6. Reviewing endings
Take off the *-ing* ending and write the root word. (For some words you may have to add a final *-e*. For some words you may have to take off a letter.)

making	make
shedding	shed
writing	write
thinking	think
taking	take
hugging	hug
bringing	bring
dipping	dip
coming	come

34

Practice 7-D: Contrasting Short Vowels e and i

i	**bill**	**lit**	**pick**	**him**	**big**	**miss**
e	**bell**	**let**	**peck**	**hem**	**beg**	**mess**

1. Write the letter.

1. pig
   peg
   p _i_ g

3. bid
   bed
   b _e_ d

5. pin
   pen
   p _e_ n

2. will
   well
   w _e_ ll

4. lid
   led
   l _i_ d

2. Circle the word that you hear.

1. bit (bet)   4. big (beg)   7. rid red   10. pick (peck)   13. tin)ten

2. (till) tell   5. (wit) wet   8. (lit) let   11. (fill) fell   14. (pit)pet

3. (chick) check   6. him (hem)   9. miss (mess)   12. six (sex)   15. bill(bell)

3. Write the short vowel that you hear.

1. y _e_ t   4. w _i_ ll   7. l _e_ d   10. d _e_ n   13. s _e_ ll

2. h _i_ p   5. p _e_ g   8. th _i_ ck   11. p _e_ p   14. k _i_ ss

3. d _e_ ck   6. w _i_ n   9. r _i_ m   12. _i_ tch   15. f _i_ n

4. Circle the right word.

1. Did you get the (bill) for the dress?
   bell

2. Jill wants ___ apples.
   tin
   (ten)

3. She will (pick) the big ones.
   peck

4. I want to go with (him) .
   hem

5. You will (miss) us when we go.
   mess

6. (Let) me go with you.
   Lit

35

Practice 7-E: Contrasting Short Vowels e and u

u	bud	hum	lug	pup	duck	but
e	bed	hem	leg	pep	deck	bet

1. Write the letter.

1. chuck
   check
   ch _e_ ck ✔

3. pup
   pep
   p _u_ p

5. duck
   deck
   d _u_ ck

2. bug
   beg
   b _u_ g

4. nut
   net
   n _u_ t

2. Circle the word that you hear.

1. (hum) hem   4. (muss) mess   7. duck (deck)   10. (pun) pen   13. mush (mesh)
2. bug (beg)   5. (bud) bed   8. (lug) leg   11. (nut) net   14. (chuck) check
3. jut (jet)   6. pup (pep)   9. but (bet)   12. dun (den)   15. (bun) Ben

3. Write the short vowel that you hear.

1. p _e_ t   4. m _u_ g   7. t _u_ b   10. b _u_ s   13. m _e_ t
2. b _u_ ck   5. l _e_ ss   8. p _u_ ff   11. f _e_ d   14. p _e_ g
3. k _e_ g   6. b _u_ t   9. wh _e_ n   12. r _u_ sh   15. g _u_ m

4. Circle the right word.

1. He is sick, (but) he will get well.
   bet

2. Put some (mush) in the dish.
   mesh

3. Bun
   (Ben) and Rick are fishing.

4. The little girl has a (pup).
   pep

5. Put some (nuts) in the fudge.
   nets

6. The man sits in his dun (den).

36

Practice 7-F: Review Lesson - Short e

1. Look at the picture and say the word. Then fill in the right letter to make the word.

 sh
_ch_ ess
ch

 ne _ck_ ck
t

 g
_j_ et
j

 d
_d_ eck
p

 she _ll_ d
ll

 t
_t_ en
d

2. Circle the word that makes sense in the sentence.

1. Ned has not met my sister ____ .
   wet
   (yet)

2. Fred yells, "This shed is a ____ !"
   less
   (mess)

3. Ed will cut the hedge for seventy ____ .
   (cents)
   sent

4. Jess (fell) and hurt his leg.
   fed

5. The children (beg) Mother for a pet.
   peg

6. The vet will check my ____ snake.
   peck
   (pet)

3. Look at the picture and say the word. Then circle the right word.

1.    peg   beg   leg   (keg)

4.   tell   (tent)   sent   ten

2.   (yell)   yet   shell   well

5.   fed   shell   bed   (shed)

3.   hem   then   (hen)   when

6.   bet   bed   (bell)   hell

37

49

Practice 7-F: Review Lesson - Short e (continued)

4. Look at the picture and say the word. Then write the word under the picture.

net   well   pen

bed   check   leg

5. Circle all the words that are the same as the first. Work from left to right.

peck	(peck)	pick	beck	(peck)	deck	(peck)	pet
ten	hen	(ten)	tent	then	tell	(ten)	net
less	chess	sell	(less)	led	(less)	let	mess
bed	(bed)	bet	deb	bell	(bed)	bud	led
wet	met	vet	(wet)	well	(wet)	met	yet
leg	led	(leg)	beg	get	lug	keg	(leg)
sell	(sell)	set	less	(sell)	well	cell	(sell)
them	then	(them)	hem	then	met	the	(them)

6. Read these sentences.

1. Peg tells me, "Ted is sick, but he will get well."

2. Yes, the men sell fresh eggs there.

3. Ken led his friends to the edge of the river.

4. Meg fed her kids. Then the kids went to bed.

5. Ed sits in the den looking at the TV set.

6. This pen has red ink. It sells for twelve cents.

7. If you make the best guess, you win the bet.

8. When Bess makes jelly, she lets the kids help her.

38

Practice 8-A: Word Family -at

1. bat

cat

-at

2. Write the letter or letters and say the word.

	at			at
b	_b_ at	p	_p_ at
c	_c_ at	r	_r_ at
f	_f_ at	s	_s_ at
h	_h_ at	ch	_ch_ at
m	_m_ at	th	_th_ at
		P	_P_ at

3. Read the words.

hat	at	chat
mat	fat	rat
pat	that	cat
bat	Pat	sat

4. Write the word you hear.

1. _fat_
2. _sat_
3. _at_
4. _pat_
5. _rat_
6. _chat_
7. _bat_
8. _cat_
9. _Pat_
10. _that_
11. _mat_
12. _hat_

5. New Words

shall   take

Word from skill book 1

Cal

6. Read the sentences.

1. I will take this hat, not that one.

2. Pitch it, and I will hit it with the bat.

3. Bess and Pat like to chat on the telephone.

4. There is mud on that mat.

5. That cat is getting fat.

   Shall I take the cat to the vet?

6. Cal sat on my hat.

7. There are rats in that shed.

8. That dress will not fit if I get fat.

9. That bat has big wings.

10. Do not put fat in the sink.

11. Pat sells cats at her pet shop.

12. The pup sat on the mat.

13. Cal pats my hand.

14. Shall I take that bat to my brother?

15. She wants to chat with Cal.

16. Bud is fat, but he wants to be thin.

17. Shall we chat for a little bit?

39

Practice 8-B: Word Family -an

1.
an

man

pan

-an

2. Write the letter or letters and say the word.

	an	t	*t* an
b	*b* an	v	*v* an
c	*c* an	th	*th* an
f	*f* an	D	*D* an
m	*m* an	J	*J* an
p	*p* an	N	*N* an
r	*r* an	V	*V* an

3. Read the words.

fan	tan	pan
ran	can	Jan
man	Van	ban
van	an	than
Dan	Nan	

4. Write the word you hear.

1. *pan*
2. *van*
3. *tan*
4. *Jan*
5. *an*
6. *ban*
7. *fan*
8. *Nan*
9. *can*
10. *ran*
11. *man*
12. *Van*
13. *than*
14. *Dan*

5. Review Words

cannot   black   stand

New Words

as   by

Word from skill book 1

Ann

6. Read the sentences.

1. Jan is standing by the fan.
2. Put an egg into the pan of water.
3. Jan has a big tan van.
4. Nan does as well as she can.
5. Ann can fix the kitchen fan.
6. Dan ran as well as the other man.
7. Jan cut up an apple and put it in the pan.
8. Dan gets as much sun as Pat.

    But Dan is less tan than Pat.
9. Did you yell to him as he ran by?
10. There is a ban on fishing. You cannot do it.
11. The red van ran into the tan truck.
12. This set of pans sells for less than that set.
13. Get a can of black olives.
14. The man is so sick that he cannot stand up.
15. Can you take the big fan there in the van?
16. I sit out in the sun and get a tan.
17. You can set the dish by the pans.

40

Practice 8-C: Word Families -am, -ab

1.   Sam   cab

   -am   **-ab**

2. Write the letter or letters and say the word.

	am		c	_c_	ab
d	_d_ am	d	_d_ ab
h	_h_ am	g	_g_ ab
j	_j_ am	j	_j_ ab
r	_r_ am	l	_l_ ab
y	_y_ am	n	_n_ ab
P	_P_ am	t	_t_ ab
S	_S_ am

3. Read the words.

jam	dam	tab	nab
Pam	ram	jab	gab
am	yam	cab	lab
Sam	ham	dab

4. Write the word you hear.

1. _ham_   9. _cab_
2. _dam_   10. _lab_
3. _ram_   11. _gab_
4. _yam_   12. _dab_
5. _am_   13. _tab_
6. _Sam_   14. _nab_
7. _Pam_   15. _jab_
8. _jam_

5. Review Words

back   family   building

New Word

keep

6. Read the sentences.

1. Sam takes a cab and gets there quickly.
2. Pam is fixing this ham for her family.

   They will have yams with the ham.
3. Do you want some jam?

   Yes, I will have a little dab.
4. Help me! I am in a jam!
5. I am building a big dam at the river.

   The dam will keep back the water.
6. Pam makes pills in the lab.
7. She puts on a pin, and it jabs her finger.
8. Did the cab ram into the truck?
9. They will nab the man when he gets there.
10. We get ham from pigs.
11. Pam is keeping tabs on her husband.
12. They are gabbing on the telephone.
13. We keep rats at the lab.
14. Cabs and trucks are in a jam on this street.
15. Pam and Jim are fishing at the dam.

41

Practice 8-D: Word Families -ack, -ax

1.   back   wax

       Jack   **-ax**

       -ack

2. Write the letter or letters and say the word.

b _b_ ack   qu _qu_ ack
j _j_ ack   sh _sh_ ack
l _l_ ack   J _J_ ack
p _p_ ack
r _r_ ack   ax
s _s_ ack   t _t_ ax
t _t_ ack   w _w_ ax
bl _bl_ ack   M _M_ ax

3. Read the words.

tack	pack	tax
sack	black	wax
rack	Jack	ax
shack	back	Max
jack	quack	
lack		

4. Write the word you hear.

1. _pack_   9. _rack_
2. _sack_   10. _Jack_
3. _jack_   11. _black_
4. _back_   12. _ax_
5. _quack_   13. _Max_
6. _lack_   14. _wax_
7. _tack_   15. _tax_
8. _shack_

5. New Words

pay   car

6. Read the sentences.

1. Max will jack up his car.
2. We must pay our tax.
3. Go out to the shack and get the ax.
4. Did she pack her black dress?
5. Max is waxing his car.
6. Put the apples into a big sack.
7. Sam hits Jack on the back. Jack's back hurts.
8. Tack up this picture.
9. Jack will pay for the black car.
10. She puts the dress back on the rack.
11. I went to the shop for a box of tacks.
12. The jack is in the back of the car.
13. She lacks ten cents to pay for the gum.
14. Can you pay me back?
15. The ducks are quacking.
16. Jack gives me a pack of gum.
17. The can of olives is in that sack.
18. Jack put the car on the rack to fix it.

42

Practice 8-E: Word Families -ag, -ad

1.   bag   bad

        tag   dad

        -ag   **-ad**

2. Write the letter or letters and say the word.

b	_b_ ag			ad
g	_g_ ag			
l	_l_ ag	b	_b_ ad	
n	_n_ ag	d	_d_ ad	
r	_r_ ag	h	_h_ ad	
s	_s_ ag	l	_l_ ad	
t	_t_ ag	m	_m_ ad	
w	_w_ ag	p	_p_ ad	
sh	_sh_ ag	s	_s_ ad	

3. Read the words.

tag	wag	mad	had
gag	shag	bad	dad
lag	rag	pad	lad
bag	sag	ad	
nag		sad	

4. Write the word you hear.

1. _sag_   10. _had_
2. _rag_   11. _dad_
3. _tag_   12. _mad_
4. _shag_   13. _sad_
5. _nag_   14. _bad_
6. _gag_   15. _lad_
7. _wag_   16. _ad_
8. _lag_   17. _pad_
9. _bag_

5. Review Word

seventy

6. Read the sentences.

1. Sam looks at the ads.
2. When Dad nags me, I get mad.
3. The shag rug has a pad under it.
4. They gag the man to keep him from yelling.
5. She is sad that she has no dad.
6. Look at the tags on that dress.
7. The bad man ran up to me. He had a gun!
8. Jack put the rags into a bag.
9. Your dress sags in the back.
10. Dan had bad cuts on his hands.
11. The ad says a bag of apples is seventy cents.
12. Kitty tags her sister on the back.
13. Pam rubs the wet dish with a rag.
14. A pen and a pad are by the telephone.
15. Did she pack her bags?
16. Mother gets mad if Dad just sits.
17. Jan is sad that the lad had to go.
18. Do not pat the cat when it is mad.

43

Note: Point out that *gas* is spelled with only one *s*. *Bass*,
meaning a kind of fish, is pronounced with the short
a sound.

Practice 9-A: Word Families -ap, -as, -ass

1.

cap	gas	glass
map	-as	-ass
-ap		

2. Write the letter or letters and say the word.

c	*c* ap	g	*g* as	
g	*g* ap			
l	*l* ap	b	*b* ass	
m	*m* ap	m	*m* ass	
n	*n* ap	p	*p* ass	
s	*s* ap	gl	*gl* ass	
t	*t* ap	gr	*gr* ass	
y	*y* ap			
ch	*ch* ap			

3. Read the words.

nap	gas
tap	
gap	mass
chap	grass
map	bass
lap	glass
yap	pass
cap	
sap	

4. Write the word you hear.

1.	*lap*	9.	*tap*
2.	*map*	10.	*gas*
3.	*sap*	11.	*pass*
4.	*cap*	12.	*glass*
5.	*nap*	13.	*mass*
6.	*yap*	14.	*grass*
7.	*gap*	15.	*bass*
8.	*chap*		

5. Review Words

happy   laugh   basket   wind

New Words

ask   where

6. Read the sentences.

1. The children are taking a nap.

2. Where is that city on the map?

3. I have on my red cap.

4. I ask her, "Can you pass that car?"

5. Wind and water can chap your hands.

6. I am happy my car did not run out of gas.

7. We laugh at the pup when it yaps.

8. The black cat jumps out of my lap.

9. I ask him to pass me a glass of water.

10. Our family will go to mass at ten.

11. There are gaps where things are missing.

12. He gets up from his nap to cut the grass.

13. "Where do you go to fish for bass?" I ask.

14. He puts the gas cap back on the car.

15. I look at the map on my lap.

16. The children tap on the glass.

17. They will not let you in unless you have a pass.

18. He is happy to get this basket of apples.

44

Practice 9-B: Word Families -ang, -ank

1. rang   thank

sang   sank

-ang   **-ank**

2. Write the letter or letters and say the word.

b _b_ ang   b _b_ ank
f _f_ ang   r _r_ ank
g _g_ ang   s _s_ ank
h _h_ ang   t _t_ ank
r _r_ ang   y _y_ ank
s _s_ ang   th _th_ ank
           H _H_ ank

3. Read the words.

hang	yank
rang	bank
sang	thank
gang	Hank
fang	tank
bang	rank
sank	

4. Write the word you hear.

1. _gang_   8. _tank_
2. _sang_   9. _Hank_
3. _bang_   10. _thank_
4. _fang_   11. _bank_
5. _rang_   12. _rank_
6. _hang_   13. _sank_
7. _yank_

5. Review Word

half

Word from skill book 1

number

6. Read the sentences.

1. Thanks for taking the check to the bank.
2. The telephone rang.
3. Hank is in a big gang of kids.
4. The snake has two big fangs.
5. Pam hangs up her dress.
6. The children sang and rang the bells.
7. Jan puts some fish in the tank.
8. The ship sank into the river.
9. Hang up that picture of our gang.
10. Hank yanks the bag out of my hands.
11. Thanks for cutting the grass.
12. Hank ranks number one in hits and runs.
13. A bell rang as the gang ran out of the bank.
14. I have half a tank of gas.
15. Jan cut her bangs.
16. Many pictures are hanging in the bank.
17. She sang to her kids when she put them to bed.
18. She bangs the pans when she is mad.

45

Practice 9-C: Word Families -ash, -atch, -ath

1. | cash | catch | path |
    | mash | match | math |
    | **-ash** | **-atch** | **-ath** |

2. Write the letter or letters and say the word.

	ash		atch
	ash	c _c_	atch
c _c_	ash	h _h_	atch
d _d_	ash	l _l_	atch
g _g_	ash	m _m_	atch
h _h_	ash	p _p_	atch
l _l_	ash		
m _m_	ash	b _b_	ath
r _r_	ash	m _m_	ath
s _s_	ash	p _p_	ath

3. Read the words.

dash	hatch
mash	patch
rash	catch
ash	match
hash	latch
sash	
lash	path
cash	bath
gash	math

4. Write the word you hear.

1.	_hash_	10.	_patch_
2.	_sash_	11.	_match_
3.	_cash_	12.	_latch_
4.	_rash_	13.	_hatch_
5.	_dash_	14.	_catch_
6.	_lash_	15.	_math_
7.	_gash_	16.	_path_
8.	_ash_	17.	_bath_
9.	_mash_		

5. **Review Words**

after   factory

New Word

work

6. Read the sentences.

1. After he works at the factory, he takes a bath.

2. Jan has a red rash on her hands.

3. He lit a match.

4. My pup runs up the path after a cat.

   I dash after him, but I cannot catch him.

5. Mash some yams to have with the hash.

6. Dan likes to work with numbers and do math.

   He works at the bank cashing checks.

7. The chicks will hatch from the eggs.

8. Her red hat does not match her red dress.

9. If I can catch that pup, I will give it a bath.

10. Patch the rip in the tan dress.

11. The glass cut a big gash in his hand.

12. That dress has a pretty sash with it.

    Will you pay cash for the dress?

13. He wants to catch some fish.

14. Sam ran up the path to the glass factory.

15. The latch will not catch.

46

Practice 9-D: Adding Endings

1. Adding -y to words

wind + y → windy

Bill _Billy_
itch _itchy_
hand _handy_
mess _messy_
puff _puffy_

2. Label the last three letters. Then write the word with -y.

VCC + y

jump + y → jumpy

VCC
mush _mushy_
VCC
hill _hilly_
VCC
dress _dressy_
VCC
luck _lucky_
VCC
fish _fishy_

3. Label the last three letters. Then write the word with -y.

CVC + C + y

Ken + n + y → Kenny

CVC
gum _gummy_
CVC
bag _baggy_
CVC
nut _nutty_
CVC
fun _funny_
CVC
Peg _Peggy_

4. Label the last three letters with VCC or CVC. Then write the word with -y.

CVC
Tim _Timmy_
CVC
sun _sunny_
VCC
grass _grassy_
CVC
dad _daddy_
CVC
bud _buddy_
VCC
fuss _fussy_

5. Add -y and read the word. Double the last letter if you have to.

Pat _Patty_
glass _glassy_
Dan _Danny_
pup _puppy_
chunk _chunky_
Sam _Sammy_
Ted _Teddy_
mud _muddy_

6. Take off -y and write the root word.

lucky _luck_
chilly _chill_
witty _wit_
puffy _puff_
runny _run_
messy _mess_
handy _hand_
chatty _chat_

7. Reviewing endings

Circle all the words that are the same as the first one.

puff	puffs	(puff)	puffing	(puff)	puffy	puffs	(puff)
bags	bag	baggy	(bags)	bagging	(bags)	baggy	bag
chilly	(chilly)	chills	chilling	(chilly)	chill	chills	chilling
tap	taps	(tap)	tapping	taps	(tap)	tapping	(tap)
picking	pick	picks	(picking)	picky	picks	(picking)	picky

47

Practice 9-E: Contrasting Short Vowels a and e

a	bag	fad	pack	sat	than	lad
e	beg	fed	peck	set	then	led

1. Write the letter.

1. bat
   bet
   b _a_ t

3. ham
   hem
   h _a_ m

5. tan
   ten
   t _e_ n

2. shall
   shell
   sh _e_ ll

4. bag
   beg
   b _a_ g

2. Circle the word that you hear.

1. (mass) mess   4. (fad) fed   7. (bad) bed   10. lad (led)   13. ham (hem)
2. (lag) leg   5. bag (beg)   8. shall (shell)   11. pack (peck)   14. (vat) vet
3. pat (pet)   6. pan (pen)   9. sat (set)   12. than (then)   15. lass (less)

3. Write the short vowel that you hear.

1. ch _e_ ck   4. p _a_ d   7. d _a_ b   10. j _a_ m   13. t _a_ x
2. sh _e_ d   5. _e_ dge   8. f _e_ ll   11. l _e_ d   14. h _e_ n
3. b _e_ t   6. r _a_ ck   9. w _e_ b   12. b _a_ ck   15. _a_ d

4. Circle the right word.

1. The ___ has black ink in it.
   pan
   (pen)

2. I ___ out in the sun to get a ___.
   (sat)
   set
   (tan)
   ten

3. Mother ___ the kids at six.
   fad
   (fed)

4. He makes less ___ I do.
   (than)
   then

5. She has a ___ cut on her leg.
   (bad)
   bed

6. We ___ take the sick cat to a ___.
   (shall)
   shell
   vat
   (vet)

48

Practice 9-F: Contrasting Short Vowels a and i

a	dad	lack	ham	fan	bat	nap
i	did	lick	him	fin	bit	nip

1. Write the letter.

1. wag
   wig
   w __i__ g

3. lap
   lip
   l __i__ p

5. bag
   big
   b __a__ g

2. sack
   sick
   s __a__ ck

4. pan
   pin
   p __a__ n

2. Circle the word that you hear.

1. (pack) pick   4. (fat) fit   7. (dash) dish   10. (thank) think   13. (rang) ring
2. dam (dim)   5. tack (tick)   8. rap (rip)   11. quack (quick)   14. sap (sip)
3. had (hid)   6. (bag) big   9. (mass) miss   12. (lad) lid   15. pan (pin)

3. Write the short vowel that you hear.

1. r __a__ m   4. t __i__ n   7. s __i__ ng   10. r __a__ nk   13. b __i__ d
2. h __i__ t   5. l __i__ nk   8. l __a__ b   11. b __a__ n   14. t __a__ p
3. s __a__ ck   6. h __a__ tch   9. p __i__ t   12. h __i__ s   15. s __a__ t

4. Circle the right word.

1. The little girl will take a (nap) / nip .

2. Put the lad / (lid) on that.

3. Be (quick) / quack ! Pack your (bag) / big !

4. The dress has a rap / (rip) in it.

5. (Thank) / Think you for the gift.

6. This (hat) / hit does not fat / (fit) .

49

Practice 9-G: Contrasting Short Vowels a and u

a	ran	tag	ham	rat	cab	sang
u	run	tug	hum	rut	cub	sung

1. Write the letter.

1. fan
    fun
    f _a_ n

3. hat
    hut
    h _a_ t

5. bad
    bud
    b _u_ d

2. tab
    tub
    t _u_ b

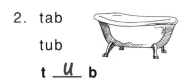

4. tack
    tuck
    t _a_ ck

2. Circle the word that you hear.

1. back (buck)   4. (mad) mud   7. (bank) bunk   10. (cap) cup   13. hang (hung)

2. (hag) hug   5. pan (pun)   8. bat (but)   11. (rag) rug   14. sack (suck)

3. cat (cut)   6. (lack) luck   9. ram (rum)   12. (badge) budge   15. (rash) rush

3. Write the short vowel that you hear.

1. n _a_ b   4. b _u_ n   7. r _a_ g   10. l _a_ g   13. h _a_ sh

2. b _u_ zz   5. j _u_ g   8. g _u_ sh   11. s _u_ nk   14. b _u_ g

3. m _a_ ss   6. c _u_ ff   9. p _a_ ck   12. s _a_ p   15. m _a_ tch

4. Circle the right word.

1. Mother yells when she gets ____ .
   (mad)
   mud

4. Put the rags in this ____ .
   (sack)
   suck

2. Dad gives his little girl a ____ .
   hag
   (hug)

5. Bill must ____ to get the bus.
   rash
   (rush)

3. Jan takes a ____ to the shop.
   (cab)
   cub

6. Jack works in the ____ .
   (bank)
   bunk

50

Practice 9-H: Review Lesson - Short a

1. Look at the picture and say the word. Then fill in the right letter to make the word.

sa _ck_ ^{g}
ck

^{v}
_f_ an
f

^{t}
ca _t_
n

^{b}
_b_ ath
p

^{l}
_t_ ag
t

^{ng}
ha _m_
m

2. Circle the word that makes sense in the sentence.

1. Bring the fan (back) / bag after you fix it.

2. The fish sang / (sank) in the tank.

3. Dad rags / (nags) at me to do my math.

4. Hank (sat) / fat on the grass by the path.

5. I am pad / (sad) to see Nan go.

6. Jack can pay the tack / (tax) . So can his bad / (dad) .

3. Look at the picture and say the word. Then circle the right word.

1.    fan (van) ran vat

2.   tax tank tag (tack)

3.   fat sat (hat) that

4.    (cab) gab cab nab

5.    bang (bank) bag ban

6.   grass gas (glass) pass

51

Practice 9-H: Review Lesson - Short a (continued)

4. Look at the picture and say the word. Then write the word under the picture.

map   can   bat

jack   grass   match

5. Circle all the words that are the same as the first. Work from left to right.

nap	pan	map	(nap)	rap	nag	(nap)	nab
sag	sad	(sag)	gag	sap	gas	wag	(sag)
mad	map	(mad)	had	dam	(mad)	mud	(mad)
ban	bang	nab	(ban)	pan	(ban)	bank	bun
dab	(dab)	dad	bad	(dab)	gab	bad	(dab)
pat	pal	tap	(pat)	bat	path	pet	(pat)
mash	(mash)	math	(mash)	mass	(mash)	sham	hash
lag	lap	(lag)	lad	gal	tag	(lag)	hag

6. Read these sentences.

1. My van ran out of gas. I will have to take a cab.

2. Jan packs a hat and a tan dress in her bag.

3. Ann Black pays cash when she shops.

    She gets a ham, a can of yams, and a sack of apples.

4. Sam had a chat with the man at the bank.

5. Pam gets mad if the cat jumps into her lap.

6. The gang sang at the mass. Did Pat thank them?

7. I will catch up to Dan's car and then pass it.

52

Practice 10-A: Word Families -ot, -on

1.

hot	on
not	Don
-ot	**-on**

2. Write the letter or letters and say the word.

c	_c_ ot	sh	_sh_ ot
d	_d_ ot	sp	_sp_ ot
g	_g_ ot		
h	_h_ ot		on
j	_j_ ot	D	_D_ on
l	_l_ ot	R	_R_ on
n	_n_ ot		
p	_p_ ot		
t	_t_ ot		

3. Read the words.

dot	got	Ron
pot	shot	Don
cot	lot	on
spot	jot	
hot	tot	
not		

4. Write the word you hear.

1. _dot_	8. _pot_
2. _got_	9. _spot_
3. _cot_	10. _shot_
4. _jot_	11. _tot_
5. _hot_	12. _on_
6. _lot_	13. _Ron_
7. _not_	14. _Don_

5. Review Words

building	Chan	doctor	Dr.
head	John	Molly	office

6. Read the sentences.

1. Don does not work a lot.
2. Molly's head is hot.
   She has red spots.
   The doctor will give Molly a shot.
3. Don has two cots in his tent.
4. Pam has on a dress with pink dots.
   Did she get a spot on her dress?
5. It got hot in the doctor's office.
6. Ron does not have any pots and pans.
7. He jots the words on a pad.
8. Ron shot a lot of ducks with his gun.
9. I sing to the little tots.
10. Did Don work out in the hot sun?
11. Dr. Chan says lots of men got sick.
12. That pot is hot. Do not pick it up.
13. She got a letter from John.
14. Ron will put up a building on that lot.

53

Practice 10-B: Word Family -op

1.   top

     shop

   -op

2. Write the letter or letters and say the word.

c _c_ op   st _st_ op
h _h_ op   sh _sh_ op
m _m_ op   ch _ch_ op
p _p_ op
t _t_ op
dr _dr_ op

3. Read the words.

mop   stop
chop   pop
top   drop
cop   hop
shop

4. Write the word you hear.

1. _shop_
2. _pop_
3. _hop_
4. _top_
5. _cop_
6. _drop_
7. _mop_
8. _chop_
9. _stop_

5. Review Words

doll   dollar

New Words

every   corn

6. Read the sentences.

1. Mop up every drop of water!

2. Stop the car! I want to get out!

3. Do not drop your dishes in the sink.

4. Jim asks Pat to chop up the eggs.

5. At the top of the hill, a girl ran into the street.

   A red car hit the girl, but it did not stop.

   The cops are looking for the car.

   They are stopping every red car in the city.

6. Her hands are wet, and she drops a dish.

7. The cops are keeping the men back.

8. Every kid likes to pop corn.

   The corn pops when it gets hot.

   Keep the top on the pan when the corn pops.

9. She pays six dollars for the doll in the shop.

10. Molly is chopping up nuts for the fudge.

11. After Bill fell, he had to hop on one leg.

12. If I drop this glass of pop, I must mop it up.

13. Ann is shopping for ham, chops, and corn.

54

Practice 10-C: Word Families -ob, -od

1.   Bob   rod

    job   **-od**

-ob

2. Write the letter or letters and say the word.

c _c_ ob   c _c_ od
j _j_ ob   n _n_ od
m _m_ ob   p _p_ od
r _r_ ob   r _r_ od
s _s_ ob   G _G_ od
B _B_ ob

3. Read the words.

rob   rod

mob   nod

job   cod

sob   God

Bob   pod

cob

4. Write the word you hear.

1. _job_   7. _nod_
2. _mob_   8. _pod_
3. _cob_   9. _cod_
4. _sob_   10. _rod_
5. _Bob_   11. _God_
6. _rob_

5. Review Words

Tom   lock

New Word

Mom

Word from skill book 1

Robert

6. Read the sentences.

1. Robert wants some corn on the cob.
2. Mom will hang the wet socks on racks.
3. Robert nods his head at Mom.
4. Bob is looking at TV.
5. Mom tells her children that God is good.

   She tells them to thank God.
6. Kim will give him a fishing rod.

   He wants to fish for cod.
7. A man robs the bank.
8. Bob got a job in the city.

   Then Tom said to Bob, "Help me get a job."
9. Pam is sad. She is sobbing.
10. There is a mob at the factory.

    The men and women want jobs.
11. We are having corn on the cob for dinner.
12. Bob asks Pat, "Will you go with me?"

    Pat nods her head.
13. Tom locks the shop so that no one can rob it.

55

Practice 11-A: Word Families -ock, -ox

1.   lock   box

        rock   **-ox**

        -ock

2. Write the letter or letters and say the word.

d _d_ ock   ox

l _l_ ock   b _b_ ox

m _m_ ock   f _f_ ox

r _r_ ock

s _s_ ock

cl _cl_ ock

sh _sh_ ock

3. Read the words.

rock   box

lock   ox

shock   fox

dock

mock

clock

sock

4. Write the word you hear.

1. _sock_   6. _rock_

2. _dock_   7. _clock_

3. _shock_   8. _fox_

4. _mock_   9. _box_

5. _lock_   10. _ox_

5. Review Words

better   father   said   skirt
stopped   was   were

New Word

o'clock

6. Read the sentences.

1. Pat will get a shock if you tell her that!

2. The kids pick up pretty rocks at the river.

3. He ran by as quick as a fox.

4. The ship will be at the dock at ten o'clock.

5. Jill put the skirts and socks in the box.

6. They were sitting on a big rock by the river.

7. Is there a clock in the kitchen?

8. The fox got the hen. I shot at the fox.

9. That man is as big as an ox.

10. Don locks up the shop at five o'clock.

11. Father said to his little son, "Put your socks on."

12. I got a shock when I was fixing the TV.

13. Jan rocks her little girl.

14. My clock has stopped. Is it six o'clock yet?

15. Tom can box better than Bob.

16. This lock works better than the other one.

56

Practice 11-B: Adding Endings (-ed)

1 Adding -ed to VCC words

T. says: There is a way to show that things have happened, that the action is *past*.

You can add *-ed* to your action word.

The *-ed* on the end of the action word tells you that something happened, that the action is in the *past*.

First we will add *-ed to* some Vowel-Consonant-Vowel words.

We hear /ed/ when we add *-ed* to words that end with the sounds /t/ and /d/.

Want ends with the sound /t/, so if we add *-ed* to it, we hear /want ed/.

Read *wanted*. [S: /want ed/] Good.

Sometimes you hear /d/, and not /ed/. (Point to *burned*.)

This word sounds like /burnd/, not /burn ed/.

Read *burned*. [S: /burnd/] Good.

Sometimes the *-ed* ending sounds like /t/ instead of /d/.

If a word ends with the sounds /k/, /f/, /p/, /s/, /sh/, /ch/, or /sk/, then the *-ed* ending will sound like /t/.

(Point to the word *help*.) *Help* ends with the sound /p/, so *helped* sounds like /helpt/. Read *helped*. [S: /helpt/] Good.

Now add *-ed* to these words and read them.

Help S. if necessary.

2 Adding -ed to CVC words

Remind S. that CVC stands for Consonant-Vowel-Consonant. Follow the same procedure as for part 1. Remind S., if necessary, that he must double the last consonant with words that end with CVC.

3 Adding -d to words that end in -e

T. says: If a word ends with an *-e*, you don't add another e. Just add the *-d*.

4 Add -d or -ed and read the words. Double the last letter if you have to.

T. says: Remember that if a word ends with an *-e* already, just add *-d*, not *-ed*.

Write these words and add *-d* or *-ed* to them.

Remember to double the last letter before adding *-ed* to words that end with Consonant-Vowel-Consonant.

Read the words that you have written.

5 Add -ed or -d to the word and fill in the blank. Double the last letter if you have to. Read the sentence.

T. says: Add *-ed* or *-d* to the action word that comes before the sentence.

Write that word in the blank. Remember to double the last letter before adding *-ed* if the word ends with Consonant-Vowel-Consonant.

Then read the sentence.

Note: Be sure S. can read *burn*.

Practice 11-B: Adding -ed or -d to Action Words to Show Past Action

1. Adding *-ed* to VCC words

   v c c + e d

   w a n t + e d ⟶ **wanted**
   b u r n + e d ⟶ **burned**
   h e l p + e d ⟶ **helped**

   Add *-ed* and read the word.

   work   *worked*
   jump   *jumped*
   ask   *asked*
   hunt   *hunted*

2. Adding *-ed* to CVC words

   c v c + c + e d

   c h a t + t + e d ⟶ **chatted**
   b e g + g + e d ⟶ **begged**
   s h o p + p + e d ⟶ **shopped**

   Add *-ed* and read the word.

   sob   *sobbed*
   tap   *tapped*
   hop   *hopped*
   spot   *spotted*

3. Adding *-d* to words that end in *-e*

   l i v e + d ⟶ **lived**
   l i k e + d ⟶ **liked**

   Add *-d* and read the word.

   judge   *judged*
   whistle *whistled*
   nudge   *nudged*
   live   *lived*

4. Add *-d* or *-ed* and read the words. Double the last letter if you have to.

   pass   *passed*
   tap   *tapped*
   like   *liked*
   rock   *rocked*
   chat   *chatted*
   burn   *burned*
   yank   *yanked*
   pat   *patted*

5. Add *-ed* or *-d* to the word and fill the blank. Double the last letter if you have to. Read the sentence.

   1. check   I *checked* my work.
   2. live   We *lived* on a hill.
   3. lock   Molly *locked* the box.
   4. nod   Father *nodded* his head.
   5. like   Jack *liked* his work.
   6. rob   Two men *robbed* the shop.
   7. hatch   The chicks *hatched*.
   8. rub   Mom *rubbed* my back.
   9. pass   That car *passed* me.
   10. stop   The cop *stopped* the car.
   11. can   Mom *canned* the corn.
   12. mess   They *messed* up the kitchen.
   13. chop   I *chopped* the olives.
   14. shock   Bob *shocked* me.
   15. beg   The pup sat up and *begged*
   16. match   Her dress *matched* her bag.

57

70

Practice 11-C: Contrasting Short Vowels a and o

a	an	cab	sack	tap	hat
o	on	cob	sock	top	hot

1. Write the letter.

1. map
   mop
   m _a_ p

3. pat
   pot
   p _o_ t

5. ax
   ox
   _a_ x

2. rack
   rock
   r _o_ ck

4. cab
   cob
   c _a_ b

2. Circle the word that you hear.

1. (rat) rot   4. shack (shock)   7. cat (cot)   10. (mad) mod   13. lack (lock)
2. (cap) cop   5. jab (job)   8. (tap) top   11. (ax) ox   14. (Dan) Don
3. pad (pod)   6. (sad) sod   9. rack (rock)   12. hat (hot)   15. chap (chop)

3. Write the short vowel that you hear.

1. c _a_ n   4. m _o_ b   7. h _o_ p   10. p _o_ t   13. s _o_ ck
2. H _a_ nk   5. t _a_ ck   8. r _o_ d   11. r _a_ n   14. s _a_ p
3. l _a_ p   6. c _a_ sh   9. t _a_ b   12. t _o_ t   15. m _a_ d

4. Circle the right word.

1. The ___ runs after the men.
   cap
   (cop)

2. I have a good ___ at the factory.
   jab
   (job)

3. A red dress is hanging ___ the ___.
   an   (rack)
   (on)   rock

4. Jan is happy, not ___.
   (sad)
   sod

5. Your ___ is sitting on my ___.
   (cat)   (hat)
   cot   hot

6. He will ___ that with an ___.
   chap   (ax)
   (chop) ox

58

Practice 11-D: Contrasting Short Vowels u and o

u	cub	hut	duck	rut	pup
o	cob	hot	dock	rot	pop

1. Write the letter.

1. luck
   lock
   l _o_ ck

2. nut
   not
   n _u_ t

3. cup
   cop
   c _u_ p

4. suck
   sock
   s _o_ ck

5. cut
   cot
   c _o_ t

2. Circle the word that you hear.

1. nut (not)   4. (hut) hot   7. (run) Ron   10. pup (pop)   13. duck (dock)
2. shuck (shock) 5. cut (cot)   8. mud (mod)   11. jut (jot)   14. cub (cob)
3. (rub) rob   6. (sub) sob   9. (shut) shot   12. (hunk) honk   15. (suck) sock

3. Write the short vowel that you hear.

1. m _o_ m   4. b _u_ t   7. j _u_ g   10. m _o_ p   13. p _o_ t
2. t _u_ ck   5. j _o_ t   8. r _u_ t   11. h _u_ t   14. c _o_ p
3. g _o_ t   6. r _o_ ck   9. d _o_ ck   12. r _u_ n   15. ch _u_ ck

4. Circle the right word.

1. That man wants to   rub / (rob)   the shop.

2. Dr. Hill will give Tom a   shut / (shot) .

3. The (pup) / pop jumps into the mud.

4. It was   hut / (hot)   in the kitchen.

5. Put the (cup) / cop in the sink.

6. He does (not) / nut have good (luck) / lock.

59

72

Practice 11-E: Review Lesson - Short o

1. Look at the picture and say the word. Then fill in the right letter to make the word.

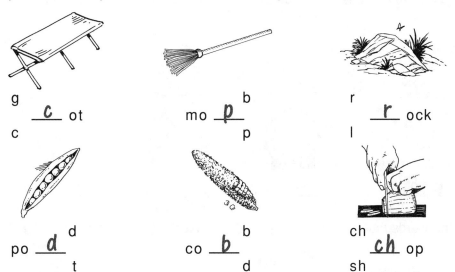

g
__c__ ot
c

p
mo __p__ b
p

r
__r__ ock
l

po __d__ d
t

b
co __b__ b
d

ch
__ch__ op
sh

2. Circle the word that makes sense in the sentence.

1. We must (stop) spot the car!

4. What a shock! Bob is quitting his jot (job) !

2. We will have corn on the (cob) cop .

5. Get rid of the robbing (rotting) apples.

3. The lots (tots) take naps at two o'clock.

6. Tom works at his dad's shot (shop) .

3. Look at the picture and say the word. Then circle the right word.

1. chop   mop   (hop)   shop

4. fox   (box)   pox   pot

2. (lock)   rock   sock   lot

5. cob   cod   (cop)   cot

3. dot   spot   pod   (pot)

6. (hot)   lot   not   rot

60

4. Look at the picture and say the word. Then write the word under the picture.

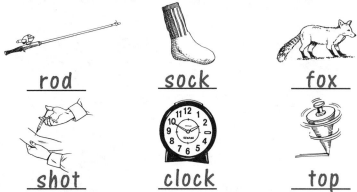

<u>rod</u> <u>sock</u> <u>fox</u>

<u>shot</u> <u>clock</u> <u>top</u>

5. Circle all the words that are the same as the first. Work from left to right.

got	(got)	jot	tot	get	pot	(got)	cot
pot	cot	(pot)	jot	pet	(pot)	got	(pot)
top	pot	stop	(top)	tot	(top)	hop	pot
god	gob	(god)	dot	pod	(god)	cod	(god)
lock	(lock)	lick	clock	(lock)	lack	luck	(lock)
spot	pot	stop	(spot)	shot	pots	(spot)	stop
box	fox	ox	(box)	ox	(box)	fox	fox
nod	rod	(nod)	don	(nod)	not	mod	(nod)

6. Read these sentences.

1. Ron pays half a dollar for a can of pop.

2. Bob is at the dock. He is fishing with his rod.

3. Don has not had the top job.

4. John shot at the fox.

5. Ron does not lock up the cash box in the shop.

   A man robs the shop.

6. The mob was mad at the cops.

7. Molly drops a cup of water. Mom mops it up.

61

74

Practice 12: Adding -es to Words

1

T. says: You have added -s to many action words.

And you have added -s to words that name person's, places, or things to make them more than one.

But there are some words you can't just add -s to, when you want to put the -s ending on a word. You must add -es, not -s.

You must add -es to words that end with -s, -x, -sh, and -ch. (Point to these letters at the top of the page.)

Listen to the sound -es makes when I add it to words with each of those endings.

Kiss, kisses; fix, fixes; dish, dishes; match, matches.

All of these are hissing sounds. (Point to the letters at the top of the page again.)

It's hard to say the sound /s/ after them, so you add a vowel sound with the -s.

It sounds like /uz/ and it's spelled e-s.

2 -s words

Add -es to these words. Fill in the blanks. Read the sentences.

T. says: Look at these words. (Point to all the *s* words.)

They all end with -s, so you have to add -es on the end.

What is this word? (Point to first word.) [S: kiss]

Now write *kiss* with the -es ending on it in the blank. [S. writes *kisses*.] Good.

How do you read it? [S: kisses] Good.

Now read the whole sentence.

Go over the words and sentences in part 2, and then parts 3, 4, and 5. Be sure S. reads the words with -es ending correctly. The ending is pronounced like /uz/ and it gives the word another syllable.

3 Take off the -es and write the root word. Read the words.

T. says: Here are some words with -es endings. Read the words.

Then take off the -es and write the root word. Read the word you have written.

Go through the words, making sure S. pronounces all the words correctly. You and the student may want to use the words in sentences as nouns or verbs.

Practice 12: Adding -es to Words

1.

-s
-x
-sh
-ch

+ es, not s

k i s s + e s ⟶ kisses
f i x + e s ⟶ fixes
d i s h + e s ⟶ dishes
m a t c h + e s ⟶ matches

2. **-s Words**

Add -es to these words.
Fill in the blanks. Read the sentences.

1. kiss   Jim __kisses__ his girl.
2. guess   I will give you two __guesses__
3. fuss   Ed __fusses__ when he is sick.
4. mess   My son __messes__ up the tent.
5. glass   I like my pink __glasses__
6. dress   Pam gets two new __dresses__
7. pass   A big car __passes__ my car.

3. **-x Words**

Add -es to these words.
Fill in the blanks. Read the sentences.

1. ax   We have two __axes__ in the shed.
2. box   She sent me two __boxes__ of fudge.
3. fix   Jan __fixes__ a duck dinner.
4. tax   We pay so many __taxes__ !
5. fox   The __foxes__ ran after the hens.
6. mix   Meg __mixes__ the chip dip.
7. wax   Dan __waxes__ his new truck.

4. **-sh Words**

Add -es to these words.
Fill in the blanks. Read the sentences.

1. dash   Kim __dashes__ after the pup.
2. wish   She __wishes__ for a black car.
3. ash   The shed burns to __ashes__.
4. rush   Mom __rushes__ out of the kitchen.
5. cash   Tom __cashes__ his check.
6. dish   Jack brings the __dishes__ to the sink.
7. mash   Nan __mashes__ the yams.
8. fish   Bud __fishes__ in the river.

5. **-ch Words**

Add -es to these words.
Fill in the blanks. Read the sentences.

1. pitch   Fred __pitches__ to us.
2. hatch   The chick __hatches__ out of the egg.
3. ditch   The men are digging big __ditches__
4. match   Take the __matches__ from the kids.
5. rich   He wants __riches__ .
6. patch   Bess puts some __patches__ on her skirt.
7. catch   Ken __catches__ the pup.
8. itch   Chuck's hand __itches__ .

6. Take off the -es and write the root word.
Read the words.

catches   __catch__
rushes   __rush__
mixes   __mix__
passes   __pass__
ditches   __ditch__
wishes   __wish__
taxes   __tax__
kisses   __kiss__
rashes   __rash__

62

Practice 13-A: Adding -er or -r to Words

1. Adding *-er* to VCC words

VCC + e r
t h i c k + e r ⟶ thicker

Add *-er* and read the words.

rich   richer

black   blacker

2. Adding *-er* to CVC words

CVC + C + e r
t h i n + n + e r ⟶ thinner

Add *-er* and read the words.

hot   hotter

big   bigger

3. Just add *-r* to words that end with *-e*.

l a r g e + r ⟶ **larger**

Add *-r* and read the words.

little   littler

large   larger

4. Add *-er* or *-r* to the word. Double the last letter if you have to. Read the word.

fresh	fresher
wet	wetter
large	larger
sick	sicker
red	redder
dark	darker
sad	sadder
quick	quicker
rich	richer
little	littler

5. Add *-er* or *-r* to the word and fill in the blank. Double the last letter if you have to. Read the sentence.

1. rich   He is __richer__ than I am.
2. hot   It is getting much __hotter__.
3. mad   He got __madder__ when I stopped him.
4. large   This park is __larger__ than the other one.
5. thin   This kid is __thinner__ than that kid.
6. dark   Your dress is a __darker__ red than my dress.
7. fresh   This egg is __fresher__ than that egg.
8. wet   Take this rag. It is __wetter__ than that one.
9. big   John is __bigger__ than his brother.
10. hard   This work is much __harder__ to do.
11. quick   The cat is __quicker__ than the rat.
12. up   I had a nap on the __upper__ bunk.
13. thick   This mix is getting __thicker__.
14. fat   Dad is __fatter__ than Mom.
15. red   Jill is getting __redder__ in the sun.
16. sick   Tom was __sicker__ than his brother.

63

Practice 13-B: Adding -er or -r to Action Words

1. Adding *-er* or *-r* to action words

This part <u>starts</u> the car.
It is a <u>starter</u>.

Jack <u>sits</u> with kids.
He is a <u>sitter</u>.

Pat <u>writes</u> for the paper.
She is a <u>writer</u>.

2. Adding *-er* or *-r* to action words

VCC + e r
s t a r t + e r ⟶ **starter**

CVC+C + e r
s i t + t + e r ⟶ **sitter**

+ r
w r i t e + r ⟶ **writer**

3. Add *-er* or *-r* to the words. Double the last letter if you have to. Read the words.

sell	seller
hit	hitter
help	helper
make	maker
run	runner
build	builder
farm	farmer
win	winner
think	thinker
whistle	whistler

4. Add *-er* or *-r* to the word. Double the last letter if you have to. Read the sentence.

1. sing — Billy wants to be a __singer__.
2. work — The factory __worker__ likes her job.
3. win — Peg is the __winner__!
4. bat — The __batter__ hurt his arm.
5. write — That __writer__ is very witty.
6. rock — Jan is sitting on the __rocker__.
7. rob — The cop will catch the __robber__.
8. bid — He sells the TV to the top __bidder__.
9. bank — The __banker__ looks at the checks.
10. kill — Get some bug __killer__ at the shop.

5. Some other words have double letters and *-er*. But the *-er* is part of the word. It is not an ending that is added.
Read the words. Use them to fill in the blanks. Read the sentences.

1. suffer — If pets do not have water, they __suffer__.
2. copper — They make the pans out of __copper__.
3. ladder — The man is standing on a __ladder__.
4. butter — I put half a cup of __butter__ in the fudge.
5. hammer — Hit the tack with a __hammer__.
6. dinner — We are having ham for __dinner__.
7. letter — Jim writes Pat a __letter__.
8. litter — Pick that up! Do not __litter__.
9. matter — It does not __matter__ when he comes.
10. summer — It gets very hot in the __summer__.

64

Practice 13-C: Endings for Words that End with Consonant + *y*

T. says: Here are three action words ending with *-y* (point to the words): *carry, marry,* and *hurry.*

These words have a consonant before the *-y.* (In each word, label the consonant before the *-y* with the letter C. Draw a line under this consonant.) In this practice you will learn how to add endings on words like this, words that end with a consonant + *y.*

1 Adding *-ing*

T. says: Just add *-ing* to *any* words that end with *-y. Carry* ends with *-y,* so just add *-ing* to make *carrying.* (Point to example.) The *-ing* ending adds another beat or part to the word. Can you hear it? *Carry. Carrying.*

Now add *-ing* to the word that comes before the sentence, and write the word in the blank. Then read the sentence.

Go over the sentences with S., making sure he spells the words correctly and pronounces them correctly (with the *-ing* adding another syllable to the word).

T. says: Now look at these words. They have the *-ing* ending on them.

What is this word? [S: hurrying] Good. Take off the ending, and write the root word in the blank.

What is the root word? [S: hurry] Good.

Go over the words with endings with S. to make sure he pronounces and spells the words correctly and that he understands the concept of root words.

2 Adding *-ed*

T. says: When you add *-ed* to a word that ends with a consonant + *y,* change the *y* to an *i* and then add *-ed.*

Marry ends with a consonant + *y,* so change the *y* to an *i* and add *-ed* to make *married.* (Point to example.)

Now add *-ed* to the word that comes before the sentence, and write the word in the blank. Then read the sentence.

Go over the sentences with S. Note that the *-ed* ending does not add another syllable to the word.

T. says: Now look at these words. They have the *-ed* ending on them.

What is this word? [S: carried] Good.
Take off the ending, and write the root word in the blank.
What is the root word? [S: carry] Good.

Go over the words with endings with S. to make sure he pronounces and spells the words correctly and that he understands the concept of root words.

3 Adding *-es* to action words

T. says: When you add *-s* to a word that ends with a consonant + *y,* change the *y* to an *i* and then add *-es.*

Hurry ends with a consonant + *y,* so change the *y* to an *i* and add *-es* to make *hurries.* (Point to example.)

Now add *-s* to the word that comes before the sentence, and write the word in the blank. Then read the sentence.

Go over the sentences with S. Note that the *-s* ending does not add another syllable to the word.

T. says: Now look at these words. They have the *-ies* ending on them.

What is this word? [S: carries] Good.
Take off the ending, and write the root word in the blank.
What is the root word? [S: carry] Good.

Go over the words with endings with S. to make sure he pronounces and spells the words correctly and that he understands the concept of root words.

4 Adding *-es* to show there is more than one

T. says: These are words that name persons, places, or things.

They all end with consonant + *y.*

Add *-s* to these words to make them *more than one.*

Remember to change the *y* to an *i* and add *-es.*
Fill in the blank and read the sentences.

Go over the sentences with S.

T. says: Now look at these words. They have the *-es* ending on them.

What is this word? [S: factories] Good.
Take off the ending, and write the root word in the blank.
What is the root word? [S: factory] Good.

Go over the words with endings with S. to make sure he pronounces and spells the words correctly and that he understands the concept of root words.

79

Note: Be sure S. can read *carry, marry, hurry, lily, puppy, garden.*

Practice 13-C: Endings for Words that End with Consonant + y

1. Adding *-ing*

Just add *-ing.*

c a r r y + i n g → carrying

Add *-ing* to the word and fill in the blank. Read the sentence.

Take off the ending. Write the root word.

carry   The men are <u>carrying</u> a TV set.   hurrying   <u>hurry</u>

hurry   Dr. Chan is <u>hurrying</u> to her office.   carrying   <u>carry</u>

2. Adding *-ed*

Change *y* to *i,* and then add *-ed.*

m a r r y
m a r r i + e d → married

Add *-ed* to the word and fill in the blank. Read the sentence.

Take off the ending. Write the root word.

marry   My sister <u>married</u> Ken.   carried   <u>carry</u>

carry   He <u>carried</u> the pup to the vet.   married   <u>marry</u>

3. Adding *-es* to action words

Change *y* to *i,* and then add *-es.*

h u r r y
h u r r i + e s → hurries

Add *-es* to the word and fill in the blank. Read the sentence.

Take off the ending. Write the root word.

hurry   Peg <u>hurries</u> to work.   carries   <u>carry</u>

carry   Rick <u>carries</u> the sack on his arm.   hurries   <u>hurry</u>

4. Adding *-es* to show there is more than one

Change *y* to *i,* and then add *-es.*

c i t y
c i t i + e s → cities

Add *-es* to the word and fill in the blank. Read the sentence.

Take off the ending. Write the root word.

puppy   Jill has six little <u>puppies</u>!   factories   <u>factory</u>

lily   The garden shop sells <u>lillies</u>.   families   <u>family</u>

jelly   Pam sells jams and <u>jellies</u>.   cities   <u>city</u>

Practice 14-A: Compound Words

Before discussing compound words, introduce S. to the idea of syllables.

T. says: You will soon find yourself reading bigger words.

The bigger words have two or more parts.

We call the parts *syllables*.

The *syllables* are the beats or parts you hear when you say the word.

Let me give you some examples.

These words have only *one* beat when you say them, even though there are many sounds in the word: (Clap once as you say each word.)

chill win fat gift shop truck head stop

These words have *two* beats when you say them: (Clap twice with each word.)

husband kitchen after little river apple

Each of these words has *two* syllables.

A word has a syllable *for every vowel sound you hear*.

But if it's hard for you to tell the number of vowel sounds in the word, say the word and listen to the number of beats or parts in it.

T. says: Now I will read you some words you've had in your reading.

You listen and tell me how many syllables each word has.

You can say the word after me or clap if you want to.

T. reads:
1. shell (1)	6. drink (1)	11. went (1)
2. address (2)	7. dollar (2)	12. about (2)
3. telephone (3)	8. much (1)	13. garden (2)
4. fit (1)	9. jam (1)	14. family (3)
5. basket (2)	10. Indian (3)	15. rub (1)

1 Look at these compound words:

T. says: Now you'll figure out some big words that have two or more syllables. They are called *compound words*.

Compound words are big words made out of two smaller words.

T. says: Look at the compound words at the top of the page. (Point to words.)

Can you see the two smaller words in each of the big words?

The smaller words are written next to the compound words.

In a compound word the two little words are right together with no space between them.

2 Put the two words together to make a compound word. Read the word.

T. says: Now look at these words.

Put the two smaller words together to make a compound word.

Write them in the blanks.

Read the smaller words and the compound words.

Check S.'s work as he reads the words. You may want to discuss the meanings of the words.

3 Find the two smaller words in each compound word. Write them in the blanks. Read the smaller words and the compound words.

T. says: Now look at these compound words.

Find the two smaller words in each compound word.

Write them in the blanks.

Read the smaller words and the compound word.

4 Make compound words. Match each word on the left with a word on the right. Write the compound word in the blank.

T. says: These are words you've read before.

Make a compound word with each of these words (point to the words on the left) by finding another word over here to go with it (point to the words on the right).

Write the compound word in the blank, next to the first word.

Then read the compound words you've made.

Here are some compound words for you to use if you want to make up more exercises. Some of the words have endings that S. has studied: *-er, -ing, -ed,* and *-s.*

aftermath	carsick	getup	handyman	kickback	nickname	paperback	sellout		thanksgiving	watercolor
another	checklist	godfather	hangout	kingpin	nowhere	passerby	setback		thickset	wedlock
anything	clockwork	godmother	hardtop		nutshell	password	setup			whereas
	cutback	godsend	hardworking	letterhead		pickax	shipbuilder	undercover		whiplash
backdrop		goodwill	hatbox	letup	oncoming	pickup	shopkeeper	undergo		windbag
backhand	deadpan	grasshopper	headquarters	linkup	onlooker	pigheaded	shoplift	underpass		windchill
backup	dishwater	gumdrop	headset	litterbug	outcome	pigpen	shotgun	undertake		windmill
bedpan	dockworker	gunshot	henpeck	lockout	outfit	pillbox	sickbed	underwater		within
bellhop			hilltop	locksmith	outlook	pinup	someone	upbringing		without
blackbird	everything	halfback	hotbed	lockup	output		somewhere	upcoming		withstand
blackout		handbag		lookout	outset	riverbank	standby	upset		workout
blacktop	farmhand	handbill	income		outskirts	riverbed	standout	upshot		workshop
buttercup	fingertip	handcuff	input	madman	outstanding	rubberneck	sunglasses	upstanding	
bypass	firsthand	handstand	intake	markup	outwit		sunspot	upstart	

Practice 14-A: Compound Words

1. Look at these compound words:

sunset	sun	set	forget	for	get	checkout	check	out
anyone	any	one	dishrag	dish	rag	backpack	back	pack

2. Put the two words together to make a compound word. Read the word.

red	head	redhead	hand	out	handout
stand	by	standby	pot	luck	potluck
street	car	streetcar	back	lash	backlash
up	keep	upkeep	any	where	anywhere
bath	tub	bathtub	patch	work	patchwork
cat	nip	catnip	sun	bath	sunbath

3. Find the two smaller words in each compound word. Write them in the blanks.
Read the smaller words and the compound words.

jackpot	jack	pot	checkup	check	up
everyone	every	one	makeup	make	up
suntan	sun	tan	comeback	come	back
outfit	out	fit	dugout	dug	out
dishwater	dish	water	pigpen	pig	pen
catfish	cat	fish	something	some	thing

4. Make compound words. Match each word on the left with a word on the right.
Write the compound word in the blank. The first one is done for you.

pop	popcorn	work	quarter	quarterback	fish
bath	bathtub	corn	shell	shellfish	back
net	network	what	pad	padlock	out
some	somewhat	tub	sun	sunburn	lock
for	forgive	hill	drop	dropout	stand
up	uphill	give	under	understand	burn

66

Practice 14-B: Two-syllable words

1

T. says: You have learned to sound out many short vowel words.

This will help you sound out many big words, too.

Look at the big words below. (Point to the words.)

They have been divided into syllables.

The syllable that is in **boldface type** is the *stressed* syllable.

We hear its vowel sound "loud and clear."

Using what you have learned about sounding out words, sound out the syllables and figure out each word.

Look at this word. (Point to *public*.)

There's a *c* at the end of the second syllable. (Point to letter.)

The *c* makes the sound /k/.

How would you say the first syllable? [S:/pub/] Good.

And the second syllable? [S: /lic/] Good.

Now put them together. What's the word? [S: /*pub* lic/] Good.

Help S. sound out the syllables if necessary.

The word *public* is used as an example because S. is used to seeing the ending sound /k/ spelled with a *ck* in many one-syllable words. S. should know that the /k/ sound at the end of many two-syllable words is spelled with just a *c*.

T. says: Look at this word. (Point to *rabbit*.)

How would you say the first syllable? [S: /rab/] Good.

And the second syllable? [S: /bit/] Good.

Notice that there are two *b's* in the middle of the word.

There is a *b* in each syllable.

But when you put the syllables together and say the word, you say only one /b/ sound.

How would you say this word? [S: /*rab* bit/] Good.

Many students will be able to sound out these words without difficulty. But if S. has trouble, you can explain, with *rabbit*, for example: "The second syllable is *bit*. In the word it sounds a little different, almost like *but*. Can you sound out the word now?"

Public and *rabbit* are examples of words where the syllables divide in this way: VC/CV in the middle with the stress on the first syllable.

Model is an example of a word divided this way: VC/V in the middle with the stress on the first syllable.

Vowels in the unstressed syllables often sound much the same–something like a short *u*. The term for this sound is *schwa,* and it is shown in dictionaries looking like an upside-down *e*.

If S. has trouble with the unstressed syllables, you can explain that the vowel sound is like the short *u* sound, because the syllable is not stressed.

If the syllable is stressed, the vowel will usually have its own short sound.

2 3

Remind the student that the **boldface** syllable is the *stressed* one.

4

Help S. if necessary.

Maybe you and S. would like to write some stories yourselves, using words learned up to this point.

83

Practice 14-B: Two-Syllable Words

1. The big words below have been divided into syllables. Using what you have learned about sounding out words, sound out the syllables and figure out each word.

public   /**pub** lic/   rabbit   /**rab** bit/
model   /**mod** el/   admit   /ad **mit**/

2. Read the word first. Then read the sentence.

1.   rabbit   /**rab** bit/
     The <u>rabbit</u> is in the garden.
2.   sudden   /**sud** den/
     Did the bus make a <u>sudden</u> stop?
3.   public   /**pub** lic/
     Anyone can come to a <u>public</u> park.
4.   napkin   /**nap** kin/
     He has a <u>napkin</u> on his lap.
5.   model   /**mod** el/
     Peg will <u>model</u> the pretty dress.
6.   limit   /**lim** it/
     Jim's car is going less than the <u>limit</u>.
7.   discuss   /**dis** cuss/
     They met to <u>discuss</u> it.

3. Read the word. Fill in the blank. Read the sentence.

1.   happen   /**hap** pen/
     Did that ___*happen*___ at work?
2.   picnic   /**pic** nic/
     I will carry the ___*picnic*___ basket.
3.   witness   /**wit** ness/
     The ___*witness*___ looks at the robber.
4.   fabric   /**fab** ric/
     I cannot get the spot out of the ___*fabric*___.
5.   finish   /**fin** ish/
     You can go after you ___*finish*___ the work.
6.   habit   /**hab** it/
     She sucks on her finger. It is a bad ___*habit*___.
7.   admit   /ad **mit**/
     The robber did not ___*admit*___ that he did it.

4. A Working Woman

Review word: heard
New word: love

Nan was up on a ladder with a hammer in her hand.
She heard a car stop.
It was her best friend Jim, coming to pick her up from work.

"It is so hot I want to go to the park for a picnic dinner," Nan said.
"This job is hard work, but I have to admit the pay is good."

Jim did not like to discuss jobs and pay.
He did not have a job yet, but he was looking for one.
He liked to fix cars and trucks.

"Shut up!" he said. "It makes me mad to think you will have to pay the bills if we get married!"

Nan stopped her work and hugged Jim.
Nan said, "You will get a job! You are better at fixing cars than anyone!"

Jim hugged her and kissed her.
"Forgive me for getting so mad," he said.
"It just upsets me to think you are working and I have no job."

Nan said, "That is the limit! If I have no job and you are working, do you think I will not love you then? Loving you is a good habit. I do not want to stop!"

Jim laughed. "I do love you so!" he said.
"You make everything so funny! I am lucky that you love me.
Does it matter if I make less than you?
I will make it up to you. When I have a good job, you can just be with our kids."

"If I want to?" asked Nan.
"If you want to," said Jim.

67

Part B: Consonant Blends

This part begins with a review of the digraphs *ch*, *sh*, *th*, and *wh* at the beginning and end of words. Most of the other practices cover one or more beginning or ending consonant blends (or *r*-controlled vowels). These practices often contain an auditory discrimination exercise between the blend and similar consonant sounds. The exercises that follow in each practice are similar to those in Part A with short vowels (writing letters and saying the word, reading the words, writing the words, and reading the sentences).

Special exercises help the student distinguish between *r* and *l* in beginning blends and between words ending with *-ng* and *-nk*. There are frequent reviews of groups of similar blends. At the end of the book, special practices help the student read longer words: compound words and two-syllable words, including those ending with CC-*le* (Consonant-Consonant-*le*), such as *middle* and *simple*. The book ends with a short story that uses blend words and words with *r*-controlled vowels.

It is very important that the student learns the short vowel sounds in Part A before moving on to the consonant blends in Part B. That is because in sections I-VII that deal with beginning blends and digraphs, words are grouped by beginning letters and do not have the same vowel and consonant endings; words with all five short vowel sounds can appear together. These groups of words are unlike the other groups of words in Part A or in the other *Focus on Phonics* books because they do not rhyme. Therefore, they are more challenging to decode, and students who cannot apply their knowledge of short vowels will have trouble reading them.

85

Practice 1-A: Review of Beginning Digraphs *sh-* and *ch-*

These digraph reviews are exactly that–*reviews*. They are not intended to teach S. the digraphs, only to help him review sounds and words he is familiar with already. If S. does not know these digraphs well, you might want him to go through relevant parts of *Focus on Phonics 1: Sounds and Names of Letters* or Part A of this workbook.

Before starting a practice, read any Note at the top of the practice page. A Note gives additional special directions *for that practice only.*

1

T. says: You have seen *s-h* and *c-h* in words. In this practice, you will review words that have *s-h* or *c-h* at the beginning.

(Point to *sh*.) What sound does *s-h* make? [S: /sh/] Good.

(Point to *shop*.) What is this word? [S: shop] Good.

(Point to *she*.) And this word? [S: she] Good.

Can you hear the /sh/ sound at the beginning of those words?

Repeat the same process for *ch*. You may want to help S. pronounce the two sounds. If S. has difficulty hearing the difference between the two sounds, or if he confuses the sounds when he pronounces them, you might write out words that are the same except for the digraph, like *chip* and *ship*. Let S. see and hear the difference, and read the words. S. will get more practice discriminating between the two sounds in part 2. You might also ask S. if he can think of other words that start with *sh* and *ch*.

2 What does the word begin with?

T. says: Now I will read some words. You listen for the beginning sounds.

If the word starts with the sound /sh/, write *s-h* in the blank.

If it starts with the sound /ch/, write *c-h* in the blank.

Go over the words, reading each word at least twice, clearly and distinctly. It may help S. to repeat the words after you, but if he does, make sure he pronounces them correctly. S. should do fairly well on this practice before going on to part 3.

3 Write the letters and say the word.

T. says: What does *s-h* sound like? (Point to *sh* at top of column.) [S: /sh/]

Good. Let's review some short vowel words that begin with that sound.

(Point to *ack*.) *A-c-k* sounds like /ack/. Say /ack/. [S: /ack/]

If I write *s-h* in front of /ack/ (write the letters in), I have the sounds /sh/ and /ack/. Say those sounds as I point to them.

(Point to *sh*.) [S: /sh/] (Point to *ack*.) [S: /ack/] Good.

Can you blend those sounds together into a word?

(Help S. if he has trouble.) [S: shack] Good.

Now let's go through the rest of the words. The vowels in the words all have short vowel sounds.

You write the letters and read the word.

Follow the same procedure with *c-h*.

In parts 3 and 4, the words are grouped by both digraphs and short vowel sounds. In part 5, the digraphs and short vowel sounds are all mixed. Obviously, S. must be very familiar with consonant sounds and short vowel sounds in order to do parts 3–6.

4 Read the words.

T. says: Here are the same words that you have been making, in a new order. Read the words.

5 Write the word you hear.

T. says: Now I will read each of the words for you. Write the word you hear.

6 Read the sentences.

Note the place for new words and review words at the top. In Part B of this workbook, the only digraph review in which a *new* word is introduced is Practice 1-B. Review words are mostly from the lessons in *Laubach Way to Reading 2* or the correlated reader *City Living*. If S. has not seen the review word before or if he does not recognize it, tell him the word. Go over the review words *what* and *shall* before having S. read the sentences.

For more detailed instructions on carrying out parts 3, 4, 5, and 6, please turn to pages 11–14.

86

Practice 1-A: Review of Beginning Digraphs sh- and ch-

1.

sh-	ch-
shop	children
she	chop

2. What does the word begin with?

      sh   **ch**

1. *ch*eek
2. *ch*ore
3. *sh*oe
4. *ch*eap
5. *sh*are
6. *sh*out
7. *ch*erry
8. *sh*in

9. *ch*ief
10. *sh*atter
11. *sh*eet
12. *ch*op
13. *ch*eer
14. *sh*ock
15. *sh*ip
16. *ch*ose

3. Write the letters and say the word.

sh		ch	
sh	ack	*ch*	at
sh	ed	*ch*	eck
sh	ell	*ch*	ess
sh	ip	*ch*	ick
sh	ock	*ch*	ill
sh	op	*ch*	in
sh	ot	*ch*	ip
sh	ut	*ch*	op

4. Read the words.

shot	chill
shock	chip
shop	chick
shut	chin
shack	chat
ship	chop
shell	chess
shed	check

5. Write the word you hear.

1. *chip*
2. *shop*
3. *check*
4. *shut*
5. *shell*
6. *chat*
7. *shock*
8. *chop*
9. *chin*
10. *shack*
11. *chill*
12. *chick*
13. *shot*
14. *chess*
15. *ship*
16. *shed*

6. Read the sentences.
Review words: what, shall

1. Do not get a chill out there.
2. The children shop for a chess set.
   Dan will write a check to pay for it.
3. Shell the nuts and chop them up.
4. That family lives in a little shack.
   There is a shed in back of the shack.
5. Ed checks the deck of the ship.
6. I shipped the gift when I got the check.
7. Ann chats with a woman in the shop.
8. The hen is with her chicks.
9. What a shock! A man robbed the shop!
10. Shall I shut up the shop?
11. Ted fell and hit his chin.
12. The cup has a chip in it.
13. The hurt man is going into shock.
    Dr. King will give him a shot.

68

87

Practice 1-B: Review of Beginning Digraphs *th-* and *wh-*

This practice has no auditory discrimination exercise. In the instructions below, the unvoiced sound of *th,* as in *thank,* is indicated by /th/. The voiced sound of *th,* as in *this,* is indicated with underlining: /<u>th</u>/.

1

T. says: In this practice, you will review words that have *t-h* or *w-h* at the beginning.

(Point to *thank.*) What is this word? [S: thank] Good.

(Point to *th.*) In *thank, t-h* has the sound /th/. Say /th/. [S: /th/] Good.

Let's look at some more words in which *t-h* has the sound /th/ at the beginning.

Have S. read through the words, assisting him if necessary.

Go to the next set. Have the student write the letters *th* in each blank and say each word. Follow the same procedure as for part 3 of Practice 1-A.

T. says: (Point to *this.*) What is this word? [S: this] Good.

(Point to *th.*) In *this, t-h* has a different sound: /<u>th</u>/.

In most words, *t-h* has the sound /th/, as in *thank.*

But in some words, like *this, t-h* has the sound /<u>th</u>/.

Let's review some words in which *t-h* has the sound /<u>th</u>/.

Have the student read *the, they, there.* Then, go to the next column. Have the student write the letters *th* in each blank and say the word. Follow the same procedure as for part 3 of Practice 1-A.

T. says: (Point to *wh.*)

You know several words that start with *w-h. W-h* has the sound /wh/.

This is a lot like the *w* sound /w/, but it has more breath to it.

You let out a puff of air as you say the sound /wh/.

(Point to *whistle.*) What is this word? [S: whistle]
(Point to *when.*) And this word?   [S: when]
(Point to *where.*) And this word?   [S: where]
(Point to *what.*) And this word?   [S: what]

Can you hear the *w-h* sound /wh/ at the beginning of the word?

That *w-h* sound is a little different from the *w* sound.

(Write down the words *witch* and *which.*)

Can you hear the difference in the beginning sounds of *witch* (point to word) and *which* (point to word)?

Say the words *witch* and *which* a few times in random order, and have the student point to the word you are saying. If the student cannot hear the difference between the two sounds, do not worry about it or continue trying to emphasize the /wh/ sound.

Go to the next column. Have the student write the letters *wh* in each blank and say each word. Follow the same procedure as in Practice 1-A for this section and for the rest of the practice.

2 Read the words.

T. says: Here are the same words that you have been making, in a new order. Read the words.

3 Write the word you hear.

T. says: Now I will read each of the words for you. Write the word you hear.

4 Read the sentences.

The new word *their* is introduced in this part. (New words are usually used at least three times in the sentences.) Explain the difference in spelling and meaning between the homonyms *their* and *there.* Use the two words in sentences.

88

Practice 1-B: Review of Beginning Digraphs th- and wh-

1. th-

thank th

_th_ ank

_th_ ick

_th_ in

_th_ ing

_th_ ink

th-

this th

the _th_ an

they _th_ at

there _th_ em

_th_ en

_th_ is

_th_ us

wh-

whistle wh

when _wh_ en

where _wh_ ip

what _wh_ ich

2. Read the words.

thin	then	which
thick	them	whip
thing	thus	when
think	that	
thank	than	
	this	

3. Write the word you hear.

1. that
2. thin
3. thus
4. them
5. thing
6. whip
7. thank
8. this
9. thick
10. when
11. than
12. which
13. think
14. then

4. Read the sentences.
New word: their
Review words: where, what, happen

1. Whip this mix. Then it will get thick.

2. Where do they live? They live there.

3. Which rug shall we get?

   A thick one is better than a thin one.

4. Thanks for thinking of me.

5. When Bob is ten, then Ted will be six.

6. What is that thing in the grass?

   Is it a whip? No, I think it is a snake.

7. What happened to their son?

8. That family has no cash in the bank.

   Thus, they cannot get their car fixed.

9. I will thank them for their gifts.

10. Jan is thinner than her sister.

11. Where do you think the kids went?

12. Which car is best? Which one do you want?

13. What things will you tell them?

69

Practice 2-A: Review of Ending Digraph –ch

1

T. says: You have seen c-h before in words.

In this practice, you will review words that have c-h at the end of words.

(Point to ch.) What sound does c-h make? [S: /ch/] Good.

It makes the same sound at the end of the word as it does at the beginning of a word.

(Point to catch.) What is this word? [S: catch] Good.

Catch has the c-h sound /ch/ at the end.

Notice that there is a t that comes before c-h in the word catch.

(Underline t in catch.) The t is silent–you don't really hear it.

Most short vowel words that end with the c-h sound /ch/ have a t before the c-h.

(Point to much.) What is this word? [S: much] Good.

This word ends with c-h, but there is no t before the c-h.

You might ask S. if he can think of other words that end with c-h or t-c-h.

2 What does the word end with?

T. says: Now I will read some words. You listen for the ending sounds.

If the word ends with the sound /ch/, write c-h in the blank.

If it ends with the sound /sh/, write s-h in the blank.

Go over the words, reading each word at least twice, clearly and distinctly. It may help S. to repeat the words after you, but if he does, make sure he pronounces them correctly. S. should do fairly well on this practice before going on to part 3.

3 Write the letters and say the word.

T. says: What does c-h sound like? (Point to ch at the top of the column.) [S: /ch/]

Good. Let's review some words that end with that sound.

(Point to bat.) B-a-t sounds like /bat/. Say /bat/. [S: /bat/]

If I write c-h after /bat/ (write the letters in), I have the sounds /bat/ and /ch/. Say those sounds as I point to them.

(Point to bat.) [S: /bat/] (Point to ch.) [S: /ch/] Good.

Can you blend those sounds together into a word?

(Help S. if he has trouble.) [S: batch] Good.

When the sounds are blended together to make the word batch, the t is actually silent. Now let's go through the rest of the words.

The vowels in the words all have short vowel sounds.

You write the letters and read the word.

Go through the words. Call attention to the last four words, which are spelled with just c-h at the end, not t-c-h.

4 5 6

Do parts 4-6 as described in the instructions on pages 95–97. In part 5, use which and witch in sentences so that if S. cannot hear the difference, he will know what word to write.

90

Practice 2-A: Review of Ending Digraph -ch

1.   -ch

catch

much

2. What does the word end with?

ch   sh

1. lea**sh**
2. lat**ch**
3. crut**ch**
4. swi**sh**
5. hu**sh**
6. mar**sh**
7. dit**ch**
8. ca**sh**
9. mu**sh**
10. bu**sh**
11. hat**ch**
12. wa**sh**
13. wit**ch**
14. poa**ch**
15. ma**sh**
16. bat**ch**

3. Write the letters and say the word.

ch   ch

bat **ch**   hit **ch**

cat **ch**   pit **ch**

hat **ch**   wit **ch**

lat **ch**   not **ch**

mat **ch**   ri **ch**

pat **ch**   whi **ch**

it **ch**   mu **ch**

dit **ch**   su **ch**

4. Read the words.

pitch	catch
ditch	hatch
itch	match
witch	batch
hitch	such
notch	much
latch	which
patch	rich

5. Write the word you hear.

1. _match_
2. _rich_
3. _batch_
4. _such_
5. _notch_
6. _catch_
7. _ditch_
8. _hatch_
9. _which_
10. _itch_
11. _latch_
12. _pitch_
13. _much_
14. _hitch_
15. _witch_
16. _patch_

6. Read the sentences.
Review words: curtains, dark, four, kitchen

1. I will pitch and you can catch.
2. Jack's hands are red. They itch.
3. Bill is such a good singer.
4. My kitchen is much bigger than yours.
5. If Ed wins the match, he will be rich.
6. Mom put a patch on the rip in my dress.
7. We want to catch a big batch of fish.
8. Dan is rich. He has four cars.
9. Which eggs will hatch?
10. The curtains do not match the rug.
11. Pam digs a ditch for the water.
12. The latch lifts into this notch.
13. The witch has a black cat with her.
14. John lit a match in the dark.
15. Is there a hitch on your car?
16. Which factory makes such good cars?

70

Practice 2-B: Review of Ending Digraphs *-sh* and *-th*

This practice covers two ending digraphs: *sh* and the unvoiced sound of *th*. The only word S. has had that ends with the *voiced* sound of *th* is *with*. S. will not study other such words until later, when he learns long vowel words.

1

T. says: You have seen *s-h* and *t-h* before in words.

In this practice, you will review words that have *s-h* and *t-h* at the end.

(Point to *sh*.) What sound does *s-h* make? [S: /sh/] Good.

It makes the same sound at the end of the word as it does at the beginning of a word.

(Point to *fish*.) What is this word? [S: fish] Good.

Can you hear the *s-h* sound /sh/ at the end of *fish*?

Let's review some short vowel words that end with the sound /sh/.

Go directly to part 2. Do the first column, following the procedure in part 2 of practice 2-A. Then return to part 1.

T. says: (Point to *th*.) You remember that *t-h* has two sounds, /th/ and /th/.

Most short vowel words that end with *t-h* end with the sound /th/.

Those are the words you will study. Say the sound /th/. [S: /th/]

Good. (Point to *path*.) What is this word? [S: path]

Can you hear the *t-h* sound /th/ at the end of *path*?

Let's go over some short vowel words that end with the sound /th/.

(Go on to the second column of part 2.)

3 4 5

Do all the remaining parts of this practice as you have done before.

Practice 2-B: Review of Ending Digraphs -sh and -th

1.   -sh   -th
     fish   path

2. What does the word end with?

s sh	t th
1. mis_s_	1. pa_t_
2. di_sh_	2. pa_th_
3. hu_sh_	3. ba_th_
4. ga_s_	4. ba_t_
5. ga_sh_	5. ma_t_
6. kis_s_	6. ma_th_
7. mas_s_	7. wi_th_
8. ma_sh_	8. wi_t_

3. Write the letters and say the word.

sh	sh	th
a _sh_	ma _sh_	ba _th_
ca _sh_	ra _sh_	ma _th_
da _sh_	di _sh_	pa _th_
fi _sh_	wi _sh_	
ga _sh_	hu _sh_	
ha _sh_	ru _sh_	
la _sh_		

4. Read the words.

wish	rash
dish	ash
fish	hash
rush	gash
hush	lash
dash	path
mash	math
cash	bath

5. Write the word you hear.

1. _hash_	9. _wish_
2. _dish_	10. _math_
3. _bath_	11. _dash_
4. _gash_	12. _lash_
5. _rash_	13. _fish_
6. _hush_	14. _cash_
7. _mash_	15. _rush_
8. _path_	16. _ash_

6. Read the sentences.
Review words: fresh, Smith, burn

1. Fill the dish with nuts.
2. They rush to the bank to cash a check.
3. Fred has a red rash on his hands.
4. Ed takes a bath after his factory work.
5. Can you help Ted with his math?
6. The pups dash up the path.
7. My kids rush into the kitchen, yelling. I tell them to hush.
8. Ted Smith is fixing hash for dinner.
9. I wish we had some fresh fish.
10. The glass cut a gash in her arm.
11. We wish to pay cash for the TV set.
12. Lash the bags to the top of the car.
13. It burned to black ashes.
14. Mash the yams for dinner.
15. Fish is the dish that Mom makes best.

71

Beginning Blends Practices

The directions and dialog that follow for Practice 3 give you a general pattern to follow for all of the beginning blends practices. You do not have to follow the dialog exactly, but make sure you are very familiar with it and with the suggestions before you begin.

Before starting a practice, read any Note at the top of the practice page. A Note gives additional special directions *for that practice only.*

1

Part 1 introduces each beginning blend. Often S. has not studied words with these blends before

T. says: This word is *lock.* (Point to first word.) Read *lock.* [S: lock]

Good. (If you know S. has learned these words before, you might ask, "What is this word?" instead of telling him.)

Lock starts with the letter *l,* so the first sound is /l/.

And this word is *block.* (Point to *block.*) Read *block.* [S: block]

The word *block* is just like *lock,* except it has the letter *b* before it. The letter *b* makes the sound /b/, and *l* makes the sound/l/, and when they come together at the beginning, you blend the sounds together to sound like /bl/. Say /bl/. [S: /bl/] Good.

T. says: What is this word? (Point to first word.) [S: lock]

And this word? (Point to second word.) [S: block]

Can you hear the extra /b/ sound in *block*?

Can you hear the *b-l* making the sounds /bl/ at the start of the word?

(Help S. go over these examples again if he has trouble.)

We call the *b-l* together a blend.

You blend the sounds of the letters together to sound like /bl/.

You will see this blend in many words. (Point to the letters of the blend *bl* at the top.)

Repeat the same process with the next words, *less* and *bless.* For the beginning *s* blends (Practices 7 and 17-22), prolong the *s* sound somewhat as you pronounce the words.

If a practice covers more than one consonant blend, you may want to introduce the first blend and then go directly to part 2, having S. do the auditory discrimination exercise in part 2 for that blend. Then return to part 1 again and introduce the next blend, following with part 2 for that blend. When S. has covered parts 1 and 2 for each blend, go on to part 3. After you have gone over each blend, you might ask S. if he can think of other words that start with that blend.

Practice 3: bl-

1. bl-

lock	less
block	bless

2. What does the word begin with?

b   l   bl

1. **bl**ouse   9. **bl**ast
2. **b**oat   10. **b**ed
3. **l**and   11. **bl**oom
4. **bl**ind   12. **l**ink
5. **bl**eed   13. **b**ond
6. **b**ank   14. **l**ame
7. **l**eak   15. **bl**ow
8. **l**ight   16. **b**each

3. Write the letters and say the word.

bl		bl	
bl ack		**bl** ock	
bl ank		**bl** ot	
bl ed		**bl** otch	
bl ess		**bl** uff	
bl ink		**bl** ush	

4. Read the words.

bless	blink
bled	blush
blot	bluff
blotch	blank
block	black

72

2 What does the word begin with?

T. says: Now I will read some words. You listen for the beginning sounds.

If the word starts with the sound /b/, write *b* in the blank.

If it starts with the sound /l/, write *l* in the blank.

But if you hear the sound of *b* and *l* blended together, /bl/, write *b-l* in the blank.

Go over the first few words with S. to make sure he knows what to do. Read each word at least twice, clearly and distinctly. You may want to emphasize the beginning sound. It may help S. if he repeats the words after you. S. will have to listen carefully, as many of the words have been chosen because they have minimal pairs; for example, *bleed* is a good word to practice because S. must be able to tell it from *bead* and *lead*.

You should check S.'s work as you go along. S. should do well on this exercise before going on to part 3. If S. seems to have difficulty with this exercise, you should give him more practice with this blend before continuing with the other exercises on this page.

Important: It is assumed that the student has a good knowledge of individual consonant sounds and short vowel sounds. If he does not, he may have difficulty with the remaining parts (3-6) of these practices. You may need to teach or review short vowel sounds for those students needing more practice. Part A of this workbook is recommended for this purpose.

3 Write the letters and say the word.

In this part, S. will be adding the beginning blend to a word stem made up of a short vowel plus a consonant or consonant digraph. The words are usually grouped together by their short vowel sounds.

T. says: What does *b-l* sound like? (Point to *bl* at top of column.) [S: /bl/]

Good. You can make new words that sound like /bl/ at the beginning.

(Point to *ack*.) *A-c-k* sounds like /ack/. Say /ack/. [S: /ack/]

If I write *b-l* in front of /ack/ (write the letters in), I have the sounds /bl/ and /ack/. Say those sounds as I point to them.

(Point to *bl*.) [S: /bl/] (Point to *ack*.) [S: /ack/] Good.

Can you blend those sounds together into a word?

(Help S. if he has trouble.) [S: black] Good.

Now let's go through the rest of the words.

The vowels in the words all have short vowel sounds.

You write the letters and read the words.

You probably won't have to follow such a detailed procedure with each word. Students who know their sounds and who can blend sounds easily may automatically write down the letters and say the words. Or they may write down the letters and instantly recognize the words without having to blend sounds together. Some students may have great difficulty with this exercise, though. You may need to follow a different procedure in helping them decode the words. For suggestions to help these students, see Appendix C: Helping Students Decode Words with Blends.

The word lists include some common names. S. should be able to identify them immediately by the capital letters. In part 3, only the words that are names have the blends already filled in in S.'s book. Make sure S. does not use capital letters as he writes the beginning blends for the other words. In a few practices, a word is both a name and a common word (example: *Frank, frank*). Words like that are listed both ways in parts 3, 4, and 5.

As S. sounds out the words, you may want to talk about them. You may want to use the words in sentences or phrases that indicate their meanings. If there are several words in a practice whose meaning S. does not know, or if S. has difficulty learning so many words all at once, you may want to circle only the most common words for him to learn. (This is especially true for English as a Second Language students.) If you decide to omit some words in part 3, you should skip over them in parts 4 and 5, too.

4 Read the words.

T. says: Here are the same words that you have been making, in a new order. Read the words.

As in part 3, the words are grouped together by short vowel sounds, although they are in a new order. If there is more than one blend being studied, the blends are kept separate as they were in part 3.

If S. is learning only part of the word lists, skip over the words he is omitting. Check his reading. Help him if he has any problems (see Appendix C for suggestions). If he has great difficulty with part 4, you should not go on with the practice. Give S. more exposure to those words later, perhaps in a different context.

5 Write the word you hear.

In this part, the words are all mixed, no longer separated by vowel sounds or even by different blends (unless the blends sound exactly alike, as for example, *sc* and *sk*).

T. says: Now I will read each of the words for you. Write the word you hear. (If S. is skipping some words in parts 3 and 4, skip them here too.)

Read the words slowly and distinctly. Repeat them as many times as necessary. S. may want to repeat a word after he hears it. If he misspells part of a word, read the word again, emphasizing the sounds he missed (the beginning, the vowel sound, the ending). For example, if he writes *black* for *block*, you may say, "The vowel sound is different. *Block. Block.*" If S. still has difficulty when you emphasize the sound, you may say, "The vowel sound is /o/. What vowel makes the sound /o/?" Tell S. when the word is a name so he can use a capital letter. Check his capitalization. You may want to help him with his handwriting, too.

You may want to emphasize part 5 for students who are new readers or poor spellers. You can use part 5 as a basic spelling program in which students can learn to spell many words easily. After S. has done a few of the blends practices, you may give him a sheet of paper and ask him to write down words with several blends mixed up together. Then he can review words he has trouble with.

6 Read the sentences.

Review words and new words that will appear in the sentences are listed at the top. Review words are mostly from the lessons in *Laubach Way to Reading 2* or the correlated reader *City Living*. Students who have gone through Part A of this workbook will also be familiar with most of these words. If S. has not had a review word before, or if he does not recognize it, *tell* him the word.

New Words are usually used at least three times in the sentences.

T. says: Here are some new words you will need in your reading. This word is . . .

Go over the review words and the new words, talking about what they mean and using them in sentences. Point out things to help S. remember the words. Have him write these words. If S. has difficulty remembering or spelling a word, put it on a flashcard for him to review frequently. S. should know these words fairly well before reading the sentences.

It is assumed that S. can read common sight words and short vowel words such as he might encounter in skill books 1 and 2, the correlated readers, and Part A of this workbook. In parts 3-5 of the blends practice, S. has had practice reading and writing certain blend words. S. should now be able to read meaningful sentences with the blend words, using the new words, review words, and words he has previously learned.

---

5. Write the word you hear.

1.	blank	6.	blotch
2.	blot	7.	bluff
3.	blush	8.	bless
4.	block	9.	black
5.	blink	10.	bled

6. Read the sentences.
Review word: name

1. Ted fills in the blanks.
2. He says he can win, but he is bluffing.
3. A black family lives in my building.
4. I get red when I blush.
5. Do not blink when I put the drops in.
6. Mom asks God to bless this dinner.
7. Tim's hand got cut. It bled a lot.
8. The gun shot blanks.
9. The black van is blocking our car.
10. Tom blushes when Pam winks at him.
11. Sam blots up the black ink.
12. Write your name in this blank.
13. "God bless you," Dad said to his son.
14. Fred lives two blocks from me.
15. Bob has a red blotch on his neck.
16. My friends are a blessing to me.

Several of the blend words have more than one meaning, so the sentences may suggest new meanings of words that you can discuss. You may need to explain some word or sentence meanings to S. if he seems confused. If he is skipping over some of the words in the word lists, you should omit the sentences that have those words until such time as he has learned the words.

In a very few practices, not all the blend words in the word lists are used in the sentences. This is because the words are less common, or because it is too difficult to make sentences with the words available.

Some students may read the sentences with great ease. For others, the sentences will be a challenge. As S. reads the sentences, note the following:

— Does he see the connections between the words he has learned and the sentences he is now reading?

— Does he recognize the most basic sight words easily? Does he need additional practice with some important words?

— Does he know the blend words well? Can he recognize them instantly, or must he sound them out? If he sounds out the words, can he do this well? What methods does he use in decoding words? Does he confuse some words with some other similar words, especially words that differ only in the vowel? What words will he still need practice with? Does he remember words from previous practices?

— What are his skills and strengths in reading?

— Does he understand the way words are used? (Words that have several common meanings may often be used in more than one way. Occasionally, words may be used as different parts of speech, such as *block*, which is used as a noun and as a verb.)

— Does S. comprehend the whole sentence? Does he understand the different types of sentences—statements, commands, exclamations, questions? Does he notice the effect of punctuation? Does he read with expression?

S. may want to go over the sentences several times until he can read them easily. Any student who wants to improve his spelling and handwriting can also *write* the sentences as you dictate them. Because the sentences contain many words from previous practices, S. may first want to review the spellings of the sight words and the blend words he has already had. When he can spell these words easily, he can go on to write the whole sentences. If S. still has trouble with some words when he writes them, you can have him write the words in a list or on cards to review.

If S. writes the sentences, call attention to the use of capital letters for the first word of every sentence and for people's names.

Remember that there is no ideal amount of time recommended for these blends practices. One student may spend several days on one practice, and another may use it as a review and spend ten minutes on it. You must adapt the practices to the needs of your individual students.

Some students may struggle with blending sounds together, decoding words, or spelling words because they have not developed phonemic awareness skills. See Appendix A: Phonics, Phonemic Awareness, and the Process of Reading, for ideas to help these students.

Practice 4: cl-

1. cl-

lock	lap
clock	clap

2. What does the word begin with?

c l cl

1. Cat
2. Cloud
3. Camp
4. luck
5. lip
6. Clash
7. Clay
8. Cause

9. leave
10. Cub
11. Clock
12. Clue
13. lean
14. lump
15. Clove
16. Cap

3. Write the letters and say the word.

cl		cl	
cl	am	cl	ip
cl	ap	cl	ing
cl	ass	cl	ock
cl	ash	cl	ot
cl	ang	cl	ub
cl	ick	cl	uck
cl	iff	cl	utch

4. Read the words.

cliff	class
cling	clap
clip	clang
click	clam
cluck	clash
club	clot
clutch	clock

5. Write the word you hear.

1. club
2. class
3. cluck
4. clip
5. clot
6. clam
7. cliff

8. clock
9. cling
10. clang
11. clash
12. clap
13. clutch
14. click

6. Read the sentences.
New words: paper, shirt
Review word: color

1. Pam clips a picture from the paper.
2. Class starts at ten o'clock.
3. They are clapping for the winner.
4. Bob is in the Garden Club.
5. Do not stand on the edge of the cliff.
6. Ed went to the river to dig for clams.
7. That red shirt clashes with this skirt.
8. The clock stopped at six o'clock.
9. Jim writes for his class paper.
10. The lock shut with a click.
11. Put the paper clips in that dish.
12. My wet shirt clings to my back.
13. The clutch on my car does not work.
14. The hens cluck at the chicks.
15. Some birds make nests on cliffs.
16. This color will clash with my shirt.

73

98

Practice 5: fl-

1. fl-

lock	lip
flock	flip

2. What does the word begin with?

f   l   fl

1. fat
2. flake
3. lint
4. lag
5. flaw
6. flute
7. fame
8. fight
9. flash
10. fare
11. loss
12. fleet
13. lick
14. lap
15. fog
16. flow

3. Write the letters and say the word.

fl   fl

fl	ag	fl	ip
fl	ap	fl	ing
fl	at	fl	ock
fl	ash	fl	op
fl	ed	fl	uff
fl	esh	fl	ush
fl	ick	fl	unk

4. Read the words.

flip	flush
fling	fluff
flick	flop
flat	flock
flash	flesh
flag	fled
flap	flunk

5. Write the word you hear.

1. flesh
2. flip
3. flock
4. flat
5. flunk
6. fled
7. flash
8. fling
9. flop
10. flag
11. flush
12. flick
13. fluff
14. flap

6. Read the sentences.
Review word: barn

1. The flag is flapping in the wind.
2. What is that flashing in the dark?
3. Tim is flat on his back in bed.
4. Flip a quarter. If it is heads, I win.
5. A flock of birds went by.
6. The farmer fled from the burning barn.
7. Bill is flunking his math class.
8. Put in the letter and lick the flap.
9. It will not flush until I fix it.
10. Jan can do a back flip.
11. Ned flops on his bed.
12. Whip the eggs until they fluff up.
13. Tom is fat. He has a lot of flesh.
14. Jack flicks on the TV.
15. The street is hilly, not flat.
16. Ann flings her ring back at Jim.

74

Note: In part 3, the beginning letters are filled in for the
      student when the word is a name and requires a capital.

Practice 6: pl-, gl-

1. **pl-**   **gl-**
   lot   lad
   plot   glad

2. What does the word begin with?

    p   l   pl   g   l   gl

1. pot   1. glaze
2. plump   2. loom
3. pant   3. gum
4. lace   4. glow
5. plead   5. goat
6. plus   6. glove
7. pain   7. land
8. ledge   8. gas

3. Write the letters and say the word.

    pl   **gl**

pl an   gl ad
pl ank   gl ass
pl edge   Gl enn
pl ot   gl um
pl us
pl uck
pl ug
pl um

4. Read the words.

plot   glum
pledge   glass
plus   glad
plum   Glenn
plug
pluck
plan
plank

5. Write the word you hear.

1. plug   7. Glenn
2. plot   8. plus
3. plan   9. glum
4. glass   10. plank
5. pledge   11. pluck
6. plum   12. glad

6. Read the sentences.
   New word: plenty

1. Plug in the TV set.
2. I cut my hand on some glass.
3. The men had a plot to rob the bank.
   We are glad that the plan did not work.
4. Peg looks glum. She misses Glenn.
5. I have plenty of planks to make a shed.
6. Bill looks good with his glasses on.
7. Glenn says the pledge to the flag.
8. Jim plucks a hen for dinner.
9. Ed plans to pledge ten dollars.
10. Kim puts the plug in the sink.
11. The Hills pick plenty of plums.
12. One plus six is seven.
13. Dad is planning his garden.
   He plans to have corn on this plot.
14. I am glad I have plenty of glasses.

75

Practice 7: sl-

1. sl-

led	lick
sled	slick

2. What does the word begin with?

        s   l   sl

1. Slope
2. lime
3. Slave
4. Sob
5. leak
6. Sang
7. Sled
8. lip
9. Slight
10. Sap
11. low
12. Sick
13. Sling
14. lump
15. Say
16. Slice

3. Write the letters and say the word.

sl		sl	
sl	acks	sl	im
sl	am	sl	ip
sl	ap	sl	ing
sl	ash	sl	ob
sl	ang	sl	ot
sl	ed	sl	ug
sl	ick	sl	um
sl	id	sl	ush

4. Read the words.

sled	slum
slot	slush
slob	slug
slam	slip
slash	slid
slap	sling
slang	slick
slacks	slim

5. Write the word you hear.

1. slot
2. slick
3. slap
4. slug
5. slim
6. sled
7. slacks
8. sling
9. slush
10. slam
11. slid
12. slash
13. slob
14. slip
15. slang
16. slum

6. Read the sentences.
New words: never, down

1. There is slush on the street.
   Do not slip on it.
2. Ann's slacks make her look slim.
3. The shop slashed rugs down to a dollar.
4. My shirt is a mess. I look like a slob.
5. Mom never slaps the children.
6. That sled will never carry four of us.
7. Pam puts on her pink slip.
8. Dr. John put Jim's arm in a sling.
9. If I slim down, my slacks will fit.
10. Put the letters in the slot.
11. Jan never lived in the city slums.
12. Don slammed down the telephone.
13. The children slip on the slick street.
14. My doctor never says slang words.
15. Ben slid down the hill on his sled.

76

Review Practices for Beginning Blends

In these practices, S. reviews a number of words he has learned for a particular group of blends. The blends being reviewed are shown at the top of the page. Much of the work involves discriminating between those similar blends.

If S. makes five or more errors on a review, he probably needs more help with those blends. It is important to note the type of error that S. makes. If S. confuses words, are they ones that *look* alike or *sound* alike? Do particular words or blends give him trouble? You may want to test him for vision or hearing problems.

After S. has completed the review practices for particular blends, you can give even more practice reviewing those words by referring immediately to Appendixes D-F. These appendixes give ideas for having S. add endings to blend words he has learned.

1 Look at the picture and say the word. Then write the letters of the beginning blend you hear.

T. says: What is this? (Point to the picture.) [S: sled] Right.

The beginning blend is missing in the word.

What are the beginning sounds in *sled*? [S: /sl/] Good.

What letters make the blend? [S: *s-l*] Good.

Write those letters in the blank.

Check S.'s work. If S. is not sure, have him pronounce *sled* very slowly, identifying the first sound, /s/, and then the second,-/l/. As you go over each of the words, make sure S. gives the right pronunciation for each word.

2 Practice the blends you have learned. Make at least 15 words with these beginnings and endings.

T. says: Now you will make some blend words.

In this column are the beginning *l* blends that you have studied. (Point to first column.)

And in this column are endings of words. (Point to second column.)

Put the beginning blends together with the word endings to make real words. The words will be ones you've seen before.

Make as many words as you can. Try to make at least 15 words.

Write the words on the lines at right.

Help S. as he makes the words. S. may want to take one beginning blend at a time, matching it with each ending to make possible words.

3 Fill in the blends to make sense in the sentences.

T. says: Here are some sentences to read. But parts of some of the words are missing. There is a space for each blend that is missing. You must fill in the right *l* blend to make words that will make sense in the sentence.

S. may immediately recognize the blend necessary to make the word that fits. Or S. may read the sentence, leaving out the word to be filled in, and try to think of the word. If S. cannot guess the word from reading the sentence, he may want to try the *l* blends one by one, to see if they make words and, if so, if the words fit. After S. fills in the correct blend, you may want him to read the sentence again.

Follow this procedure for Practice 16: Review of Beginning *r* Blends and Practice 23: Review of Beginning *s* and *w* Blends.

102

Practice 8: Review of Beginning l Blends: bl-, cl-, fl-, gl-, pl-, sl-

1. Look at the picture and say the word. Then write the letters of the beginning blend you hear.

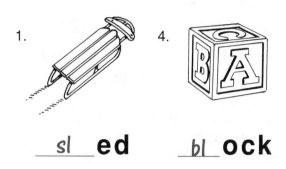

1. _sl_ **ed**

4. _bl_ **ock**

2. _cl_ **am**

5. _gl_ **ass**

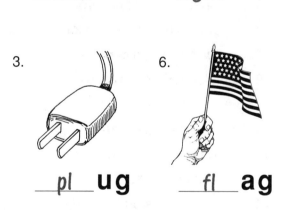

3. _pl_ **ug**

6. _fl_ **ag**

2. Practice the blends you have learned. Make at least 15 words with these beginnings and endings.

bl	ash	blot	fled
cl	ip	bled	fling
fl	ot	clash	plot
pl	ed	clip	plum
sl	um	clot	slash
gl	ing	cling	slip
		flash	slot
		flip	sled

3. Fill in the blends to make sense in the sentences.

pl   fl   gl   bl   cl   sl

1. Our class says the _pl_ edge to the flag.
2. Glenn is watching a _fl_ ock of birds.
3. There was _sl_ ush on the street. It was _sl_ ick.
   Ed slipped and fell _fl_ at on his back.
4. We are _gl_ ad you plan to visit our club.
5. Tim looks _gl_ um. He is _fl_ unking math.
6. Mom made plenty of _pl_ um jam.
7. His shirt clashes with his _sl_ acks.
8. I have lots of paper clips and _bl_ ank paper.
9. We _cl_ ap for Jan. We make her _bl_ ush.

77

Practice 9: br-

1. **br-**

ring	rag
bring	brag

2. What does the word begin with?

    b   **r**   **br**

1. bake
2. broom
3. risk
4. bride
5. roach
6. ban
7. brain
8. book

9. ridge
10. bed
11. brand
12. boil
13. brush
14. bag
15. race
16. brave

3. Write the letters and say the word.

br	**br**
br ag	br ick
Br ad	br idge
br an	br im
br ass	br ing
br at	br ush

4. Read the words.

bran	brush
brat	bring
brass	brick
Brad	bridge
brag	brim

5. Write the word you hear.

1. brush
2. brat
3. brim
4. brass
5. bring

6. Brad
7. brick
8. bran
9. bridge
10. brag

6. Read the sentences.
New words: hair, made
Review words: bread, brother, turn

1. Mom brags, "This is good bread I made."

   She made bread with bran in it.
2. Ben brushes his hair quickly.
3. I cannot carry the bricks up that hill.
4. The bridge is slick when it is wet.
5. Fill my glass to the brim.
6. I brushed the cat's hair from my skirt.
7. Kim brings me some jam for the bread.
8. This dish is made of brass.
9. My little brother is a brat.
10. Brad lives in a big brick building.
11. Bring me a glass of water.
12. The brim of his hat was turned down.
13. "My son is a doctor," he brags.
14. The red truck is on the bridge.
15. Brad has to brush up on his math.

78

104

Practice 10: cr-

1. cr-

rib	rack
crib	crack

2. What does the word begin with?

c   r   cr

1. <u>C</u>ane	9. <u>r</u>ush
2. <u>r</u>ude	10. <u>cr</u>y
3. <u>cr</u>oak	11. <u>C</u>ook
4. <u>C</u>ab	12. <u>r</u>aw
5. <u>r</u>ank	13. <u>C</u>ash
6. <u>cr</u>eam	14. <u>cr</u>ib
7. <u>cr</u>ack	15. <u>cr</u>ust
8. <u>r</u>ate	16. <u>C</u>op

3. Write the letters and say the word.

cr	cr
<u>cr</u> ab	<u>cr</u> ib
<u>cr</u> ack	<u>cr</u> op
<u>cr</u> am	<u>cr</u> ush
<u>cr</u> ash	<u>cr</u> utch
<u>cr</u> ank	

4. Read the words.

crush	crank
crutch	crack
crash	crop
cram	crib
crab	

5. Write the word you hear.

1. <u>crib</u>
2. <u>crank</u>
3. <u>crab</u>
4. <u>crash</u>
5. <u>cram</u>
6. <u>crutch</u>
7. <u>crop</u>
8. <u>crush</u>
9. <u>crack</u>

6. Read the sentences.
New word: baby

1. The baby is in his crib.
2. Ed got hurt in a car crash.
   A car crushed his leg.
   Ed is on crutches till he gets well.
3. I had to crank up the car to start it.
4. Will you crack the nuts for me?
5. The baby crushed bread in her fingers.
6. Farmers want to have big crops.
7. The brick building fell with a crash.
8. A farmer keeps his corn in a crib.
9. My best pot has a crack in it.
10. When I pack my bags, I cram things in.
    Then my things get crushed.
11. The baby drops the cup and cracks it.
12. We will sell our corn crop.
13. We had crab legs for dinner.

79

105

Practice 11: dr-

1. dr-

rip	rug
drip	drug

2. What does the word begin with?

       d   **r**   **dr**

1. **d**rown
2. **r**ag
3. **d**ive
4. **dr**ill
5. **r**um
6. **d**ear
7. **d**unk
8. **dr**aw
9. **r**aft
10. **d**ead
11. **dr**ain
12. **d**ip
13. **dr**eam
14. **d**ug
15. **r**ink
16. **dr**y

3. Write the letters and say the word.

   dr   **dr**

dr ag	**dr** ink
dr ank	**dr** op
dr ess	**dr** ug
dr ill	**dr** um
dr ip	**dr** unk

4. Read the words.

dress	drank
drop	drag
drum	drip
drunk	drink
drug	drill

5. Write the word you hear.

1. *drug*
2. *drop*
3. *drill*
4. *drink*
5. *dress*
6. *drag*
7. *drunk*
8. *drip*
9. *drum*
10. *drank*

6. Read the sentences.
New words: school, play

1. Drag the boxes out of the shed.
2. He dropped out of school to play drums.
3. Are the men drilling for water?
4. Sam drank so much he got drunk.
5. Molly's red dress is pretty.
6. Drink plenty of water.
7. That dress is dripping wet.
8. I dropped my fishing rod in the water.
9. She drank every drop of her drink.
10. This school play drags on and on.
11. Water is dripping from the sink.
12. Dr. King locks up the drugs.
13. Don plays the drums after school.
14. She keeps drilling us on our math.
15. We never dress up to go to school.
16. Ed looks drunk, but he is sick.

80

Practice 12: fr-, pr-

1. **fr-**   **pr-**

   rank   rank

   frank   prank

2. What does the word begin with?

   f   r   fr   p   r   pr

   1. rank   1. peach
   2. free   2. pray
   3. fill   3. robe
   4. fog   4. pride
   5. frame   5. pick
   6. risk   6. raise
   7. fright   7. pose
   8. fail   8. proof

3. Write the letters and say the word.

   fr   pr
   fr ank   pr ank
   Fr ank   pr ess
   Fr an   pr om
   Fr ed   pr op
   fr et
   fr esh
   fr ill

4. Read the words.

   fret   prop
   fresh   prom
   Fred   press
   Fran   prank
   Frank
   frank
   frill

5. Write the word you hear.

   1. press   7. Fred
   2. frank   8. fresh
   3. fret   9. prank
   4. frill   10. prom
   5. prop   11. Frank
   6. Fran

6. Read the sentences.
   Review words: friend, pretty, market

   1. Press down on it to make it flat.
   2. My friends played a prank on me.
   3. Fred will get some fresh eggs for us.
   4. Let me be frank. This is what I think.
   5. The baby frets for her mother.
   6. Prop the sick girl up in bed.
   7. Frank is pressing his black slacks.
   8. Fran's dress for the prom has frills.
   9. Max has a fresh fish market.
   10. The cops pressed the mob back.
   11. Do not fret if you cannot do it.
   12. The rack fell down. Prop it back up.
   13. The women are good friends.
   14. Fran has such pretty dresses!
   15. The paper goes to press at six.
   16. Get some fresh bread for dinner.

81

Practice 13: gr-

1. **gr-**

rip	ram
grip	gram

2. What does the word begin with?

g   r   gr

1. greed
2. race
3. gain
4. grab
5. gas
6. go
7. rid
8. ripe
9. graze
10. groom
11. rim
12. gate
13. grove
14. gout
15. grape
16. round

3. Write the letters and say the word.

gr

gr ab
gr am
gr ass
Gr eg
gr ill

gr

gr in
gr ip
gr it
gr ub
gr udge

4. Read the words.

grin	grudge
grill	grub
grit	grass
grip	grab
Greg	gram

5. Write the word you hear.

1. grab
2. grip
3. Greg
4. grill
5. grin
6. gram
7. grudge
8. grass
9. grit
10. grub

6. Read the sentences.
New word: grubby
Review word: ready

1. Greg grins when he is happy.
2. I grab my bag and run for the bus.
3. Does Frank like grits?
4. Ed is grubby. He fell in the mud.
5. Pat grabs his hand and grips it hard.
6. Fran will cut the grass.
7. Do not carry a grudge.
8. Digging ditches is grubby work.
9. Mom mops up the mud and grit.
10. "Grub is ready! Come and get it!"
11. The baby grins when Dad laughs.
12. Set up the grill on the grass.
    Greg wants to grill the fish.
13. I got grubby working on my car.
14. I want to grab the jug from him.
    But I cannot get a good grip on it.

82

Practice 14: tr-

1. tr-

rack	rip
track	trip

2. What does the word begin with?

t   r   tr

1. rack	9. tend
2. trail	10. trash
3. trap	11. ripe
4. tuck	12. tree
5. rust	13. tot
6. trim	14. ramp
7. rot	15. tick
8. tip	16. trace

3. Write the letters and say the word.

tr		tr	
tr	ack	tr	ip
tr	ap	tr	ot
tr	ash	tr	uck
tr	ick	tr	udge
tr	im	tr	unk

4. Read the words.

trot	trip
trunk	trim
truck	trick
trudge	
trap	
trash	
track	

5. Write the word you hear.

1. trip	6. trot
2. truck	7. track
3. trash	8. trudge
4. trim	9. trick
5. trunk	10. trap

6. Read the sentences.

1. We want to catch the rats in the trap.
2. Frank runs at the track.
3. Jack plays a trick on Don.
4. Fran will trim Pat's hair.
5. I got a dress for the trip.
   I will pack it in this trunk.
6. Mom put my shirt in the trash.
7. Do not track mud on the rug.
8. The kids trudge up the hill.
   The pup trots after the kids.
9. Trim the fat from the chops.
10. The jack is in the trunk of the car.
11. Do not trip on that trash can.
12. There are car tracks on the grass.
13. She tells her pet to do a trick.
14. That truck is carrying six pigs.

83

Practice 15: Contrasting *r* and *l*

Not all students will need this practice. It is especially designed for students who need more work with the *r* and *l* sounds. People who speak the following languages are most likely to have difficulty with the *r* and *l* sounds: Burmese, Chinese, Dutch, Hawaiian, Japanese, Korean, Micronesian, Samoan, Swahili, Thai, and Vietnamese. (See *Pronunciation Contrasts in English* by Don L. F. Nilsen and Alleen Pace Nilsen; Wareland Press, inc., 2002.) Of course, the difficulty with *r* and *l* is not limited to foreign students.

All of these people may need practice with *r* and *l* at the beginning, middle, and ending of words, but this practice will consider *r* and *l* only in beginning blends. Thus, S. will discriminate between *br-* and *bl-*, *cr-* and *cl-*, *fr-* and *fl-*, *gr-* and *gl-*, *pr-* and *pl-*.

Before starting the practice, you may want to help S. pronounce the *r* and *l* sounds individually. If he is having trouble making the sounds, you might mention that in pronouncing the *l* sound /l/, the tongue tip touches the tooth ridge. In pronouncing the *r* sound /r/, the tongue tip does not touch anything.

T. says: You have studied the beginning *l* blends and the beginning *r* blends.

Often people mix up blends when the second letter is *r* or *l*. For example, they confuse *f-r* with *f-l*. This practice will give you more work with those blends that are easy to confuse: *b-r* and *b-l*, *c-r* and *c-l*, *f-r* and *f-l*, *g-r* and *g-l*, and *p-r* and *p-l*.

1

T. says: Here are two words you have seen before.

This word is *grass*. (Point to the word.) Read *grass*. [S: grass]

Grass starts with the *g-r* blend. It sounds like /gr/ at the beginning.

Can you hear the *r* sound /r/ in the blend?

This word is *glass*. (Point to the word.) Read *glass*. [S: glass]

Glass starts with the *g-l* blend. It sounds like /gl/ at the beginning.

Can you hear the *l* sound /l/ in the blend?

Grass. Glass. Can you hear the difference in sound?

Do you see why they are spelled the way they are?

(Go over example again if S. has trouble.)

2 Look at the picture and say the word. Then circle the blend you hear. Now look at the picture and say the word.

T. says: Listen for the blend at the beginning of the word.

Then circle the blend that makes the sounds you hear.

(Help S. if he has trouble.) S. may want to repeat the words after you. If so, make sure S. pronounces the words correctly.

3 Circle the blend you hear.

T. says: Now I will read some words. You listen again for the blend at the beginning. Circle the blend that makes the sounds you hear.

Go through the first few words with S. to make sure he knows what to do. If S. repeats the words after you, make sure he pronounces them correctly. You may want to correct S.'s mistakes in part 3 before going on to part 4. You can correct mistakes as he makes them, or at the end of this part.

4 Write in *r* or *l* for each word you hear.

T. says: This time, I will read some words again, and you will listen for the beginning blend.

The word that I say is written down, except for the second letter.

You fill in that letter–either *r* or *l*–that makes the blend that you hear.

Go through the first few words with S. to make sure he knows what to do. If S. repeats the words after you, make sure he pronounces them correctly. You may want to correct S.'s mistakes as he makes them, or at the end of part 4. If S. misses five or more in either part 3 or part 4, he probably needs additional work with the *r* and *l* sounds in blends.

110

Practice 15: Contrasting r and l

1.

r

gr
grass

l

gl
glass

2. Look at the picture and say the word. Then circle the blend you hear.

(br) bl   cr (cl)   fr (fl)   (br) bl   (fr) fl

3. Circle the blend you hear.

1. fr (fl) flame	11. (br) bl braid	1. c _r_ ack	11. p _r_ op
2. gr (gl) glue	12. cr (cl) claw	2. f _l_ ock	12. c _l_ ock
3. (br) bl breed	13. gr (gl) glaze	3. p _r_ ank	13. b _l_ ush
4. pr (pl) play	14. (br) bl brew	4. b _l_ ed	14. g _r_ and
5. (cr) cl croak	15. (fr) fl fright	5. g _l_ ad	15. c _l_ ass
6. (gr) gl grade	16. (cr) cl crime	6. c _l_ amp	16. c _r_ ank
7. cr (cl) cloud	17. br (bl) bleach	7. f _r_ ank	17. f _r_ esh
8. br (bl) blight	18. (pr) pl pry	8. p _l_ od	18. g _r_ ass
9. (gr) gl groom	19. (fr) fl frail	9. b _r_ and	19. c _l_ ap
10. fr (fl) flee	20. gr (gl) glow	10. c _l_ utch	20. c _r_ ash

4. Write in *r* or *l* for each word you hear.

Note: For this review, follow procedure on page 102.

Practice 16: Review of Beginning r Blends: br-, cr-, dr-, fr-, gr-, pr-, tr-

1. Look at the picture and say the word. Then write the letters of the beginning blend you hear.

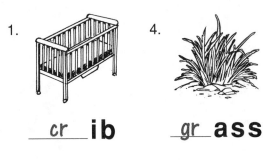

1. ___cr___ **ib**   4. ___gr___ **ass**

2. ___tr___ **uck**   5. ___dr___ **um**

3. ___br___ **ush**   6. ___br___ **idge**

2. Practice the blends you have learned.

Make at least 10 words with these beginnings and endings.

br	ank	_brag_	_drank_
cr	op	_brush_	_dress_
dr	ush	_crank_	_drip_
fr	ess	_crop_	_drop_
gr	ag	_crush_	_frank_
pr	ip	_drag_	_grip_
tr			

3. Fill in the blends to make sense in the sentences.

cr   tr   br   gr   dr   fr   pr

1. Fred _tr_ipped and fell down on the bridge.

2. My friend Greg _br_ings me some _fr_esh bread.

3. Brad's _tr_uck crashed into a van.

4. That brat likes to play tricks and _pr_anks on us.

5. Fran fixes _cr_ab and grilled fish for dinner.

6. Put the _tr_im on the edge of that dress.

   Then _pr_ess the dress. It will be ready for the _pr_om.

7. She _dr_ops the cup. It has a _cr_ack in it.

8. Never take any _dr_ugs when you are drinking.

9. Frank _gr_abs the trunk and _dr_ags it to the truck.

85

Practice 17: st-

1. st-

tack	top
stack	stop

2. What does the word begin with?

s　　t　　st

1. st ay
2. t ar
3. s ing
4. s ag
5. st ill
6. t ick
7. st eep
8. s and
9. t eam
10. st age
11. st art
12. t ab
13. s ale
14. st ack
15. s eed
16. s ave

3. Write the letters and say the word.

st	st
st ab	st ill
st ack	st itch
st aff	st ing
st an	st ink
st em	st ock
st ep	st op
st ick	st uck
st iff	st uff

4. Read the words.

stop	stick
stock	stink
staff	stitch
stab	still
Stan	stuff
stack	stuck
sting	step
stiff	stem

5. Write the word you hear.

1. stuck
2. still
3. staff
4. sting
5. stem
6. stock
7. stiff
8. stab
9. step
10. stack
11. stitch
12. stuff
13. Stan
14. stink
15. stop
16. stick

6. Read the sentences.
Review words: stand, word

1. Ed stops on the steps. He stands still.
2. Our school staff works hard.
3. My finger stings where I cut it.
4. Dad stuffs the hen with bread stuffing.
5. The fudge stuck to the pan.
6. His words were like a stab in the back.
7. I still do not have that hat in stock.
8. The tent is stiff and hard to stitch.
9. Stan keeps the buds fresh.
   He puts the stems in water.
10. Dad stacked the dishes in the sink.
11. Stop playing with that stick.
12. The apples are rotting. They stink!
13. Stan's car was stuck in the ditch.
14. Dr. Bell will stitch up the cut.
15. If your legs get stiff, stand up.

86

113

Practice 18: sp-

1. sp-

pill	pot
spill	spot

2. What does the word begin with?

s   p   sp

1. __sp__ill
2. __p__ark
3. __S__end
4. __sp__ank
5. __S__oon
6. __p__in
7. __sp__ite
8. __S__ay
9. __p__ort
10. __S__eed
11. __sp__are
12. __p__ool
13. __sp__ace
14. __sp__oke
15. __S__oil
16. __p__ot

3. Write the letters and say the word.

sp   sp

__sp__ an   __sp__ ill
__sp__ at   __sp__ in
__sp__ ank   __sp__ it
__sp__ eck   __sp__ ot
__sp__ ed   __sp__ un
__sp__ ell

4. Read the words.

spot	spank
spell	spun
sped	spit
speck	spill
spat	spin
span	

5. Write the word you hear.

1. __speck__
2. __spin__
3. __spat__
4. __spell__
5. __spun__
6. __spot__
7. __spank__
8. __spill__
9. __sped__
10. __spit__
11. __span__

6. Read the sentences.

1. Can you spell this word?
2. The hot sun makes my head spin.
3. The baby spit up on her dress.
4. Stan spilled his drink on the rug.
   He mopped up the spot with a rag.
5. Jim sped up the street in his car.
6. We made up after our little spat.
7. There are black specks on this paper.
8. Tim spits at his sister.
   Mom will spank him.
9. The baby spun the top.
10. Jack has spots on his glasses.
11. We are having a hot spell.
12. Pam spilled ink on her skirt.
13. What is the span of that bridge?
14. The hot rod spins down the track.

87

114

Practice 19: sn-

1. sn-

nag	nip
snag	snip

2. What does the word begin with?

 s n sn

1. *n*ag
2. *sn*ore
3. *s*ip
4. *n*ail
5. *sn*ack
6. *n*ear
7. *s*ub
8. *sn*eeze
9. *s*ake
10. *n*o
11. *s*ide
12. *sn*ob
13. *s*oup
14. *sn*eak
15. *n*ap
16. *s*ort

3. Write the letters and say the word.

s n		s n	
sn ack		*sn* itch
sn ag		*sn* ob
sn ap		*sn* uff
sn iff		*sn* ug
sn ip		

4. Read the words.

snip	snag
snitch	snap
sniff	snack
snug	snob
snuff	

5. Write the word you hear.

1. *snip*
2. *snuff*
3. *snap*
4. *snitch*
5. *snag*
6. *snob*
7. *snack*
8. *snug*
9. *sniff*

6. Read the sentences.
Review word: snake

1. I snap my fingers and my pup runs up.
2. That snob thinks he is better than we are.
3. I snagged my dress getting in the car.
4. Our children are snug in their beds.
5. A snake is in the tent.
6. That pup is sniffing at our ham.
7. The baby has a snack after his nap.
8. I want some snaps to put on my skirt.
9. Kim snips an ad out of the paper.
10. That shirt is a little snug for me.
11. The man is sniffing. He must be sick.
12. We have apples and nuts for snacks.
13. The snob thinks his car is best.
14. The pup snapped at my friend's leg.
15. Tom snitches his sister's apple.
16. Our plans hit a snag.

88

Practice 20: sm-

1. sm-

mash	mock
smash	smock

2. What does the word begin with?

s m sm

1. **SM**all
2. **S**oak
3. **M**elt
4. **SM**ack
5. **SM**ooth
6. **S**ight
7. **M**ug
8. **SM**art
9. **S**earch
10. **M**ile
11. **SM**ear
12. **M**other
13. **S**ock
14. **S**ell
15. **SM**udge
16. **M**ash

3. Write the letters and say the word.

sm

SM ack
SM ash
SM ell
SM ock
SM udge

4. Read the words.

smell

smock

smudge

smash

smack

5. Write the word you hear.

1. _smash_
2. _smell_
3. _smack_
4. _smudge_
5. _smock_

6. Read the sentences.
New words: smog, smart
Review words: cover, Smith

1. The car smashed into a bridge.
2. Cars and factories make smog.
3. It is smart to get a good little car.
4. Ed gives Jill a big smack on the lips.

   "You smell good to me," he says.
5. Ron has a smudge on his chin.
6. Jan puts on a smock to cover her dress.
7. The stuff in that trash can smells bad.
8. Smog covers the city.
9. Pat smacked the bug with the paper.
10. Dan Smith thinks he is so smart!
11. There is a smudge on this paper.
12. He smashed the trash down in the can.
13. It is smart to get rid of smog.
14. We can smell the dinner.

    We smack our lips.

89

116

Practice 21: sk-, sc-

1. **sk-**   **sc-**

   kid   cab

   skid   scab

2. What does the word begin with?

s	k	sk		s	c	sc
1. **S**unk				1. **SC**are		
2. **sk**y				2. **S**our		
3. **k**it				3. **C**orn		
4. **sk**ill				4. **S**ale		
5. **k**ey				5. **SC**ab		
6. **S**in				6. **S**old		
7. **sk**ate				7. **C**uff		
8. **S**ip				8. **SC**oop		

3. Write the letters and say the word.

sk		sc	
_sk_ etch		_sc_ ab	
_sk_ id		_sc_ an	
_sk_ ill		_sc_ ott	
_sk_ im		_sc_ uff	
_sk_ in			
_sk_ ip			
_sk_ it			
_sk_ unk			

4. Read the words.

skim	Scott
skit	scuff
skill	scan
skin	scab
skip	
skid	
skunk	
sketch	

5. Write the word you hear.

1. _skit_	7. _skill_
2. _skunk_	8. _skin_
3. _skip_	9. _scuff_
4. _sketch_	10. _scan_
5. _skim_	11. _Scott_
6. _skid_	12. _scab_

6. Read the sentences.
   New word: scatter
   Review words: school, mark

1. That car skids on the wet street.
2. School can help me get job skills.
3. I will sketch a picture of you.
4. The kids scatter when the bell rings.
5. I skip things when I skim a paper.
6. Pam has a new skirt for school.
7. Scott skinned his leg when he fell.
   He has a scab where his skin got cut.
8. The wind scatters her sketches.
9. Jack skipped school to go fishing.
10. Frank scans the paper quickly.
11. When skunks get mad, they smell bad.
12. Do not get any scuff marks on it.
13. Mr. Bell is skilled in fixing cars.
14. Our school will put on a funny skit.
15. There is a scatter rug by my bed.

90

Practice 22: sw-, tw-

1. **sw-**   **tw-**

   well   win

   swell   twin

2. What does the word begin with?

s	w	sw		t	w	tw
1. **W**et			1. **W**ig
2. **SW**itch			2. **T**ang
3. **S**eat			3. **TW**eed
4. **SW**ay			4. **W**ill
5. **S**ore			5. **TW**irl
6. **W**ine			6. **TW**ice
7. **SW**eep			7. **T**in
8. **S**ift			8. **TW**inge

3. Write the letters and say the word.

sw	tw
SW am	**tw** ig
SW ell	**tw** in
SW im	**tw** itch
SW itch	
SW ing	
SW ung	

4. Read the words.

swing	twin
switch	twitch
swim	twig
swell	
swung	
swam	

5. Write the word you hear.

   1. _swell_
   2. _twin_
   3. _swing_
   4. _swam_
   5. _twitch_
   6. _swung_
   7. _twig_
   8. _swim_
   9. _switch_

6. Read the sentences.
   New word: twenty
   Review words: twelve, watch

   1. Ann likes to swim in the river.
   2. The twins played on the swings.
   3. Jack swung at the bug and hit it.
   4. Twelve men and twenty women were there.
   5. Twigs and little sticks burn quickly.
   6. The twins like to switch jobs.
   7. Twenty of my friends will come.
   8. A bug bit Ed, and his hand swelled up.
   9. There are twelve eggs in that box.
   10. A school of fish swam by.
   11. Dad swings the baby up in his arms.
   12. "Your new dress looks swell," Ed said.
   13. Switch on the TV. I want to watch it.
   14. Hank swung the bat and got a hit!
   15. The pup's leg is twitching.
   16. The slacks sell for twenty dollars.

91

118

Practice 23: Review of Beginning s and w Blends: st-, sp-, sn-, sm-, sk-, sc-, sw-, tw-

1. Look at the picture and say the word. Then write the letters of the beginning blend you hear.

1.

<u>sk</u> **unk**

2.

<u>tw</u> **enty**

3.

<u>st</u> **ep**

4.

<u>sw</u> **ing**

5.

<u>st</u> **ick**

6.

<u>sn</u> **ake**

2. Practice the blends you have learned. Make at least 14 words with these beginnings and endings.

st	ell	<u>scuff</u>	<u>spell</u>
sp	itch	<u>skin</u>	<u>spin</u>
sn	in	<u>smell</u>	<u>stuff</u>
sm	ack	<u>smack</u>	<u>stitch</u>
sc	uff	<u>smock</u>	<u>stock</u>
sk	ock	<u>snack</u>	<u>swell</u>
sw		<u>snuff</u>	<u>switch</u>
tw		<u>stack</u>	<u>twin</u>

3. Fill in the blends to make sense in the sentences.

sc   sk   sm   sn   st   sw   tw   sp

1. Scott is still <u>sw</u>imming. He never <u>st</u>ops!

2. Stan <u>sp</u>ills the ink. It makes a <u>sp</u>ot on the rug.

3. That <u>sk</u>unk stinks! It <u>sm</u>ells bad!

4. My <u>tw</u>in brother <u>sw</u>ings the bat for a hit.

5. She got a <u>sm</u>udge on her sketch.

6. His car <u>sk</u>ids into the ditch. It gets <u>st</u>uck.

7. <u>st</u>itch the <u>sn</u>aps on the smock.

8. Scott skips the words he cannot <u>sp</u>ell.

9. Stan <u>sk</u>ins his arm. He gets a <u>sc</u>ab on it.

10. He has a big stock of apples for <u>sn</u>acks.

Beginning Three-letter Blends

Practices 24, 25, and 26 deal with three-letter blends and digraphs. For these practices, follow the same procedure as for other beginning blends, except for parts 1 and 2, which are slightly different. The instructions below can guide you. Refer to Practice 24, *str*.

1

T. says: You have studied most of the common two-letter blends that are at the beginning of words. In this practice, you will study a three-letter blend, *s-t-r*. In this blend, three sounds are blended together.

(Point to *rap*.) This word is *rap*. Read *rap*. [S: rap]
(Point to *t* in *trap*.) If I add the *t* sound /t/ to *rap*, the *t* sound /t/ and the *r* sound /r/ are blended together to sound like /tr/, and I get the word *trap*. Read *trap*. [S: trap]
Can you hear the difference in *rap* and *trap*?

(Point to *s* in *strap*.) Now if I add the *s* sound /s/ to *trap*, the *s* sound /s/ and the *t* sound /t/ and the *r* sound /r/ are blended together to sound like /str/, and I get the word *strap*. Read *strap*. [S: strap]
Can you hear the difference in *rap, trap,* and *strap*?

In Practice 26, the two letters of the digraphs *sh* and *th* make one sound, so you build the *shr-* and *thr-* words in two steps, not three.

2 What does the word begin with?

Part 2 of all three practices is different only in that S. will be listening for two- or three-letter blends, rather than just two-letter blends or single consonants. This will probably be more difficult for him. Make sure S. knows what he is to do.

Practice 24: str-

1. **str-**

    rap

    trap

    strap

2. What does the word begin with?

    st   **tr**   **str**

1. _str_aw
2. _tr_ain
3. _st_ate
4. _st_eam
5. _str_ike
6. _tr_ap
7. _st_ew
8. _str_eet

9. _st_and
10. _tr_ay
11. _str_ess
12. _st_ing
13. _str_ive
14. _str_ange
15. _tr_ip
16. _str_oll

3. Write the letters and say the word.

   str   **str**

str ap   _str_ uck

str ess   _str_ um

str etch   _str_ ut

str ing   _str_ ung

str ip

4. Read the words.

strip	strum
string	strap
strut	stretch
struck	stress
strung	

5. Write the word you hear.

1. _struck_
2. _strip_
3. _stress_
4. _string_
5. _strap_
6. _strum_
7. _strut_
8. _strung_
9. _stretch_

6. Read the sentences.
Review word: street

1. Ann stretches her arms and legs.
2. The kids are playing in the street.
3. This string is no good.
4. The red van struck our car.
5. Dan is under stress on his job.
6. Molly straps the pack on her back.
7. I got up when the clock struck six.
8. I have strung up the net. Let us play.
9. Ed cut the paper into thin strips.
10. This strap will stretch.
11. Tom struck a match to burn the twigs.
12. Bill strums the strings and sings.
13. The winner struts up and down.
14. We stress good spelling in our class.
15. After work, I stretch out on my bed.
16. The girl's bag hung by a strap.

93

121

Practice 25: scr-, spr-, spl-, squ-

1. **scr-**   **spr-**
    cram   ring
    scram   spring

    spl-   **squ-**
    platter   quint
    splatter   squint

2. What does the word begin with?

     scr spl spr squ

1. _scr_eam   5. _squ_are
2. _spr_ead   6. _spl_ice
3. _spl_urge   7. _spr_out
4. _scr_ape   8. _squ_eal

3. Write the letters and say the word.

    scr   **spr**
  scr am   _spr_ ang
  scr ap   _spr_ ing
  scr atch
  scr ub

    squ   **spl**
  squ int   _spl_ ash
                  spl it

4. Read the words.

  scrub   split
  scram   splash
  scratch
  scrap

  spring   squint
  sprang

5. Write the word you hear.

1. _scrap_
2. _split_
3. _spring_
4. _squint_
5. _scratch_
6. _splash_
7. _scrub_
8. _sprang_
9. _scram_

6. Read the sentences.

1. Scrub your hands after you work.
2. I write the number on some scrap paper.
3. Split the apple in two. Give me half.
4. The park is pretty in the spring.
5. I cannot stand cats that scratch me. I tell them to scram!
6. The passing car splashed mud on me.
7. This bed has no springs.
8. Mom fed the pup some scraps of ham.
9. The sun makes me squint.
10. We get our water from that spring.
11. Fred scrubs the kitchen with a mop.
12. Ben sprang out of bed at six o'clock.
13. Ted got into the tub with a splash.
14. Sam and Jill will split up.
15. Pam scratched her hand fixing her car.

94

Practice 26: shr-, thr-

1. **shr-**   **thr-**

  rug   rush

  shrug   thrush

2. What does the word begin with?

sh   r   shr   **th   r   thr**

1. <u>shr</u>imp   1. <u>th</u>ought
2. <u>sh</u>ed   2. <u>thr</u>ead
3. <u>r</u>ank   3. <u>r</u>ob
4. <u>shr</u>unk   4. <u>th</u>umb
5. <u>sh</u>oe   5. <u>thr</u>ust
6. <u>r</u>ug   6. <u>th</u>aw
7. <u>shr</u>iek   7. <u>thr</u>oat
8. <u>sh</u>ine   8. <u>r</u>ush

3. Write the letters and say the word.

  shr   **thr**

  <u>shr</u> ed   <u>thr</u> ill
  <u>shr</u> ill   <u>thr</u> ush
  <u>shr</u> ink
  <u>shr</u> ub
  <u>shr</u> ug

4. Read the words.

  shrug   thrush

  shrub   thrill

  shrink

  shrill

  shred

5. Write the word you hear.

1. <u>shrill</u>
2. <u>thrush</u>
3. <u>shrink</u>
4. <u>shrub</u>
5. <u>shred</u>
6. <u>thrill</u>
7. <u>shrug</u>

6. Read the sentences.
New word: thread
Review words: three, nurse

1. We have shrubs in our garden.
2. It thrills me when you sing!
3. I want some pink thread.
4. That shrill whistle makes my head hurt.
5. The nurse works till three o'clock.
6. My shirt is ripped to shreds.
7. I ask Kim if this dress will shrink.
   Kim shrugs and says, "What if it does?"
8. We have three children.
9. I snip a bit of thread from my shirt.
10. A thrush is singing in our garden.
11. I get a thrill out of you, baby!
12. Bob cut the paper into shreds.
13. That dress will shrink if it gets wet.
14. Where do you keep your thread?
15. The pup is digging under the shrubs.

95

123

Practice 27: Review of Beginning Blends

T. says: In this practice, you will review many of the blends you have studied.

1 Look at the picture and say the word. Then write the letters of the beginning blend you hear.

T. says: Look at the picture and say the word.

Then fill in the letters of the blend you hear.

Be sure S. pronounces each word correctly. S. fills in the missing blend that makes the sounds he hears.

2 Circle all the words that are the same as the first one.

T. says: Circle all the words that are the same as the first.

Work from left to right.

This is primarily a *visual* discrimination exercise. It is useful for giving evidence of visual problems like poor vision, directional problems, and reversals of letters and words. It is very important for you to note the kinds of errors S. makes. Some of the incorrect words are new to S., but they *look* like the word to be circled. In a few cases, an incorrect word is the same as the circled word except for the vowel. If S. makes an error by circling these words, he is probably not noticing the vowels in words. If S. makes many mistakes in this visual discrimination exercise (three or more), you should check further for visual problems.

3 Draw a line from each blend to an ending to make a word.

T. says: Now you will match some beginnings and endings of words.

The words have blends that you are reviewing.

There are two groups of words (point to each group).

First do one group of four words, and then the other.

In each group, match the beginnings with the endings to get four real words.

Draw a line from the right beginning to the right ending.

Use each beginning and ending once.

The vowels in the words all have the short sound.

(Help S. blend the sounds together to make words.)

4 Use these words to fill in the blanks.

T. says: Here are eight words that you have seen before. (Point to words.)

They have some of the blends that you are reviewing.

Read the words. (Go over the words with S. Make sure S. knows the meanings of the words also.)

Now you will use those eight words in sentences.

Read each sentence and fill in the word that makes sense.

Use each word just once.

Note: These instructions and dialog can be used exactly as is for Practice 43, Review of Other Ending Blends.

Practice 27: Review of Beginning Blends

1. Look at the picture and say the word. Then write the letters of the beginning blend you hear.

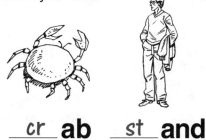

__cr__ **ab**   __st__ **and**

__tw__ **elve**   __pl__ **um**

__br__ **ick**   __sw__ **im**

2. Circle all the words that are the same as the first one.

stiff	fits	sniff	(stiff)	stuff
	(stiff)	still	(stiff)	
flap	flop	(flap)	flat	flip
	(flap)	lap	flip	
brag	(brag)	drag	(brag)	garb
	bag	grab	bran	
spin	spun	(spin)	pins	(spin)
	skin	(spin)	snip	

3. Draw a line from each blend to an ending to make a word.

fl ╳ em
gr   us
pl   esh
st   in

sk ╳ ash
bl   ug
sn   ank
tr   in

4. Use these words to fill in the blanks:

| clutch | slim | bless | brick |
| spit | twigs | trap | swell |

1. The school building is made of ___brick___.

2. The slacks make you look ___slim___ and trim!

3. He ___spit___ out the gum and put it in the trash.

4. We want God to ___bless___ this dinner.

5. You have to step on the ___clutch___ in this car.

6. We plan to catch rats with this ___trap___.

7. Pick up the ___twigs___ and little sticks.

8. The sting is making my arm ___swell___ up.

96

Ending Blends Practices

1

T. says: This word is *ten*. (Point to first word.) Read *ten*. [S: ten] Good.

Ten ends with the letter *n*, so the last sound is /n/.

And this word is *tent*. (Point to *tent*.) Read *tent*. [S: tent]

The word *tent* is just like *ten,* except it has a *t* after it.

The letter *n* makes the sound /n/, and *t* makes the sound /t/, and when they come together at the end, you blend the sounds together to sound like /nt/. Say /nt/. [S: /nt/] Good.

What is this word? (Point to first word.) [S: ten]

And this word? (Point to second word.) [S: tent]

Can you hear the extra /t/ sound in *tent*?

Can you hear the *n-t* making the sounds /nt/ at the end of the word?

(Help S. go over these examples again if he has trouble.)

We call the *n-t* together a blend.

You blend the sounds of the letters together to sound like /nt/.

You will see this blend in many words. (Point to the letters of the blend *nt* at the top.)

Repeat the same process with the next words, *plan* and *plant*, and so on.

In some practices, the contrast is between pairs like *fat* and *fast*. Follow the instructions on page 140 for contrasts like these. In Practice 32: *-ng,* the contrast is between *win* and *wing*. Tell the student that you do not add a /g/ sound to the /n/ sound to say *-ng*. The letters *-ng* together make one sound: /ng/. In Practice 33: *-nk,* the contrast is between *wing* and *wink*. Tell the student to read the letters *-nk* by saying the sound /ng/ and then adding the sound /k/.

If there is more than one consonant blend covered in the practice, you may want to introduce the first blend and then go directly to part 2 for that blend. Then return to part 1 again and introduce the next blend, following with part 2 for that blend. When S. has covered parts 1 and 2 for each blend, go on to part 3.

When pronouncing words with ending blends, you may want to emphasize both sounds of the blend at the end. For ending *s* blends, you may want to prolong the *s* sound.

2 What sound does the word end with?

T. says: Now I will read some words. You listen for the ending sounds.

If the word ends with the *n* sound /n/, write *n* in the blank.

If it ends with the *t* sound /t/, write *t* in the blank.

But if you hear the sound of *n* and *t* blended together, /nt/, write *n-t* in the blank.

Go over the first few words with S. to make sure he knows what to do. Read each word at least twice, clearly and distinctly. You may want to emphasize the ending sounds. It may help S. to repeat the words after you. S. will have to listen carefully, as many of the words have been chosen because they have minimal pairs (example: *pant* is a good word because S. must be able to tell it from *pan* and *pat*).

You may want to check S.'s work at this point. S. should do well on this exercise before going on to part 3. If S. seems to have difficulty with this exercise, you may want to give him more practice with this blend later, before continuing with the other exercises on this page.

Important: It is assumed that the student doing these practices has a good knowledge of individual consonant sounds and short vowel sounds. At this point, he should also be fairly familiar with beginning consonant blends. If he does not know all of these sounds, he may have difficulty with the remaining parts (3-6) of these practices.

3 Write the letters and say the word.

In this part, S. will be adding ending blends to single consonants, digraphs, or the consonant blends just covered, plus a vowel (having the short sound). The words are grouped together by their short vowel sounds. Words with similar short vowels and ending letters will rhyme.

T. says: What does *n-t* sound like? (Point to *nt* at top of column.) [S: /nt/]

Good. You can make new words that sound like /nt/ at the end.

The vowels in the words you will make have the *short* sound.

(Point to *a*.) *A* sounds like /a/. Say /a/. [S: /a/] Good.

If I write *n-t* after /a/ (write the letters in), I have the sounds /a/ and /nt/. Say those sounds as I point to them.

(Point to *a*.) [S: /a/] (Point to *nt*.) [S: /nt/] Good. Can you blend those sounds together into a word?

(Help S. if he has trouble.) [S: ant] Good.

Now let's go through the rest of the words.

You write the letters and read the word.

You probably won't have to follow such a detailed procedure with each word. Students who know their sounds and who can blend sounds easily may automatically write down the letters and say the words. Or they may write down the letters and instantly recognize the words without having to blend sounds together. Some students may have great difficulty with this exercise, though. You may need to follow a different procedure in helping them decode the words. For suggestions to help these students, see Appendix C: Helping Students Decode Words with Blends.

Refer to the instructions for beginning blends, pages 94–97, for more detailed directions for parts 4, 5, and 6.

Special Directions for Practices 28-B: *-nt* and 29-B: *-nd*

Both the blends *-nt* and *-nd* have two practices because of the number of words to be used. The second practices should be carried out just like the first except for part 2. In Practice 29-B, part 2 is an auditory discrimination exercise for *-nd* and *-nt*. Here are directions for part 2 of Practice 28-B, *-nt*:

2 *-nt* and *-nd* words

T. says: In the last practice, you learned these four words: *bent, lent, sent,* and *spent* (point to the words as you read them).

They are easy to confuse with four other words you will meet in the lesson after this one: b*end, lend, send,* and *spend* (point to the words). Those two sets of words sound alike, but there are differences. Listen while I read them in pairs. *Bend, bent. Lend, lent. Send, sent. Spend, spent.* Can you hear that the first word ends with the sounds /nd/, and the second word, which you know, ends with the sounds /nt/? The first word is spelled with *n-d* at the end, and the second word is spelled with *n-t* at the end.

What is the difference in each pair of words, besides ending sounds?

The first word is used to talk about things that happen in the *present,* especially things that happen again and again.

For example: We *send* letters to them. I *spend* a lot of money.

The second word talks about things that are *past*– they have happened, they are finished.

For example: She *lent* me money last week. He *bent* down.

Do you understand the difference? (Answer any questions S. may have.)

That's why it's important to notice whether these words end with *nt* or *nd.* You will see these four *nd* words again in the lesson after this one.

Practice 29-B: *-nd*

2 What does the word end with?

T. says: You have studied many *-nt* words, and you are now studying many *-nd* words. It is important to notice whether words end with *-nt* or *-nd.* I will read some words. You listen for the blend at the end. Then write *-nt* or *-nd* in the blank for each word.

Note: In part 5, use *sent* and *cent* in sentences
so S. will know which word to write.

Practice 28-A: -nt

1.   -nt

ten   plan

tent   plant

2. What does the word end with?

	n	t	nt

1. de**nt**
2. ra**t**
3. stu**n**
4. sca**n**
5. cou**nt**
6. rai**n**
7. hu**nt**
8. mi**nt**
9. spli**t**
10. te**nt**
11. pai**nt**
12. wi**n**
13. re**nt**
14. a**n**
15. fro**nt**
16. le**t**

3. Write the letters and say the word.

	nt		nt
a	**nt**	le	**nt**
pa	**nt**	re	**nt**
gra	**nt**	se	**nt**
pla	**nt**	te	**nt**
sla	**nt**	ve	**nt**
be	**nt**	we	**nt**
ce	**nt**	spe	**nt**
de	**nt**		

4. Read the words.

lent	rent
vent	tent
bent	pant
sent	slant
dent	grant
went	ant
spent	plant
cent	

5. Write the word you hear.

1. _tent_
2. _bent_
3. _pant_
4. _went_
5. _slant_
6. _cent_
7. _lent_
8. _ant_
9. _vent_
10. _dent_
11. _grant_
12. _sent_
13. _plant_
14. _rent_
15. _spent_

6. Read the sentences.
New word: aunt
Review word: twenty

1. Ben sent the rent check to Mrs. Bell.
2. I spent twenty dollars for the pants.
3. Aunt Molly sent me a gift.
4. We have a vent in our kitchen.
5. They are living in a tent by the river.
6. Twenty of us went to work at the plant.
7. I asked Aunt Peg to grant me one wish.
8. Dan was panting as he ran up the steps.
9. Scott lent her twenty cents.
10. My aunt and uncle plant a garden.
11. There are ants and bugs in the tent.
12. That picture is hung on a slant.
13. Ned and Jan are renting a truck.
14. Aunt Pam bent down to look at a plant.
15. Ed got a dent in his car.

    He spent twenty dollars to fix it.

Practice 28-B: -nt

1. **-nt**

tin	stun
tint	stunt

2. *-nt* and *-nd* words

be**nd**	be**nt**
le**nd**	le**nt**
se**nd**	se**nt**
spe**nd**	spe**nt**

3. Write the letters and say the word.

	nt		**nt**
hi	**nt**	hu	**nt**
li	**nt**	pu	**nt**
mi	**nt**	blu	**nt**
ti	**nt**	gru	**nt**
fli	**nt**	stu	**nt**
pri	**nt**		
spli	**nt**		
squi	**nt**		

4. Read the words.

blunt	lint
hunt	flint
stunt	splint
punt	mint
grunt	squint
tint	hint
print	

5. Write the word you hear.

1. *print*　　8. *squint*
2. *hunt*　　9. *stunt*
3. *tint*　　10. *mint*
4. *flint*　　11. *splint*
5. *grunt*　　12. *punt*
6. *lint*　　13. *hint*
7. *blunt*

6. Read the sentences.
New word: yard
Review words: another, want

1. I drop hints for the gift I want.
2. Print your name in this blank.
3. This dress is covered with lint.
4. The stunt man fell and hurt his arm.
   We put a splint on his arm.
5. He can kick a punt very well.
6. Birds hunt for bugs in our yard.
7. That one has a blunt edge.
8. Ann tints her hair red.
9. We will plant mint in our back yard.
10. What do you want? Give me a hint.
11. Do not squint. Put on your glasses.
12. I want some help in our yard.
13. When you shop, get me some flints.
14. The pig grunts as it hunts for nuts.
15. I want another print of this picture.

98

Practice 29-A: -nd

1. **-nd**

men   ten

mend   tend

2. What does the word end with?

      n   **d**   **nd**

1. wi**n**   9. mi**nd**
2. be**d**   10. a**d**
3. po**nd**   11. Be**n**
4. gra**nd**   12. hi**d**
5. fi**n**   13. blo**nd**
6. ha**d**   14. le**d**
7. sou**nd**   15. sa**nd**
8. te**n**   16. wi**nd**

3. Write the letters and say the word.

   nd   **nd**

e **nd**   bo **nd**

be **nd**   fo **nd**

le **nd**   po **nd**

me **nd**   blo **nd**

se **nd**

te **nd**

ble **nd**

spe **nd**

4. Read the words.

pond	send
bond	lend
blond	bend
fond	spend
mend	tend
end	blend

5. Write the word you hear.

1. tend   7. spend
2. pond   8. bond
3. bend   9. mend
4. end   10. blend
5. fond   11. send
6. lend   12. blond

6. Read the sentences.
New words: tender, money
Review word: friend

1. Bob lends me money for the trip.
2. Her hands are red and tender.
3. I send letters to friends I am fond of.
4. Mom bends down to pick up her son.
5. Jim tends to spend a lot of money.
   We must put an end to his spending.
6. Pam is mending a rip in the dress.
7. Dad sends Ed to the pond to catch fish.
8. Blend the eggs into the mix.
9. Never send money in a letter.
10. My husband says many tender things.
11. My friend Ben is very fond of blonds.
12. Ned will be happy to tend the kids.
13. They run to the end of the street.
14. Jan spends money on stocks and bonds.
15. Scott gives a tender kiss to Jan.

99

Note: Part 2 gives special practice
discriminating between *nd* and *nt*. See
directions for part 2 on page 128.

Practice 29-B: -nd

1. **-nd**

ban	win
band	wind

2. What does the word end with?

nd   nt

1. le**nd**
2. stu**nt**
3. bli**nd**
4. a**nd**
5. spe**nt**
6. be**nt**
7. fou**nd**
8. pla**nt**
9. te**nt**
10. wa**nd**
11. ki**nd**
12. se**nt**
13. bo**nd**
14. mou**nt**
15. gra**nt**
16. me**nd**

3. Write the letters and say the word.

nd   nd

a **nd**	gra **nd**
ba **nd**	sa **nd**
ha **nd**	sta **nd**
la **nd**	stra **nd**
gla **nd**	wi **nd**
bra **nd**	fu **nd**

4. Read the words.

wind	band
fund	gland
sand	hand
land	brand
and	grand
stand	strand

5. Write the word you hear.

1. land
2. stand
3. grand
4. and
5. wind
6. brand
7. gland
8. hand
9. strand
10. fund
11. band
12. sand

6. Read the sentences.
New words: grandmother, Andy

1. Jill has a wedding band on her hand.
2. This land is covered with sand.
3. Wind and water can chap your hands.
4. I can stand up, but I cannot bend down.
5. We had a grand fishing trip with Andy.
6. The school is running out of funds.
7. They cannot land in this bad wind.
8. Grandmother's school is still standing.
9. The kids are playing in the sand.
10. Andy plays drums in the band.
11. Grandmother sends us jams and jellies.
12. My car got stuck, and I was stranded.
13. I cannot stand this wind!
14. Grandmother is mending Andy's shirt.
15. Hand me that can of corn.

    I like that brand.

100

Practice 30: -nch

1. -nch

pin   bran

pinch   branch

2. What does the word end with?

  n   ch   nch

1. bru**nch**   9. cle**nch**
2. mu**ch**   10. pit**ch**
3. tre**nch**   11. lu**nch**
4. it**ch**   12. ra**n**
5. bra**n**   13. que**nch**
6. be**nch**   14. hut**ch**
7. crut**ch**   15. bu**n**
8. pu**n**   16. wret**ch**

3. Write the letters and say the word.

  nch   nch

ra **nch**   pi **nch**

bra **nch**   bu **nch**

be **nch**   hu **nch**

que **nch**   lu **nch**

dre **nch**   mu **nch**

tre **nch**   pu **nch**

i **nch**   cru **nch**

4. Read the words.

drench   crunch

trench   bunch

quench   munch

bench   pinch

hunch   inch

punch   ranch

lunch   branch

5. Write the word you hear.

1. _lunch_   8. _trench_
2. _drench_   9. _branch_
3. _ranch_   10. _munch_
4. _punch_   11. _pinch_
5. _quench_   12. _crunch_
6. _inch_   13. _bunch_
7. _bench_   14. _hunch_

6. Read the sentences.
Review word: valley

1. We have a big ranch in the valley.
2. I have a hunch that Jack wants to go.
3. I fell in the water and got drenched.
4. When I pinched her arm, she yelled.
5. A bunch of us work at a branch office.
6. Take up the pants an inch and a half.
7. Andy made some punch for our lunch.
8. The apple crunched when he bit into it.
9. The batter went back to the bench.
10. A bunch of branches fell in our yard.
11. That car missed me by inches.
12. I have a hunch I am going to win.
13. The ranch hands stop work for lunch.
14. I picked up an apple to munch on.
15. Stan punched in at seven o'clock.
16. She digs a trench in her yard.

101

Note: Tell S. that *-nce* and *-nse* make the same sound. Note that in part 2, S. works only with *-nce,* not *-nse.* In part 5, tell S. where *-nce* words stop and *-nse* words begin.

Practice 31: -nce, -nse, -nge

1.

-nce	-nse	-nge
sin	ten	twin
since	tense	twinge

2. What does the word end with?

n	nce		n	nge
1.	da**nce**		1.	bi**n**
2.	fe**nce**		2.	stra**nge**
3.	he**n**		3.	lou**nge**
4.	si**nce**		4.	spu**n**
5.	wi**n**		5.	cri**nge**
6.	cha**nce**		6.	ra**nge**
7.	pri**nce**		7.	twi**n**
8.	te**n**		8.	plu**nge**

3. Write the letters and say the word.

nce	nse	nge
da **nce**	se **nse**	hi **nge**
cha **nce**	te **nse**	fri **nge**
gla **nce**	ri **nse**	plu **nge**
tra **nce**		
fe **nce**		
si **nce**		
pri **nce**		

4. Read the words.

fence	rinse	plunge
prince	sense	fringe
since	tense	hinge
chance		
trance		
dance		
glance		

5. Write the word you hear.

1. since
2. glance
3. dance
4. fence
5. prince
6. chance
7. trance
8. rinse
9. tense
10. sense
11. fringe
12. plunge
13. hinge

6. Read the sentences.
New word: once

1. Jan puts up a fence to keep her pup in.
2. He wants a chance to dance with her.
3. I glance at the clock and rush to work.
4. Will you fix the hinge on my trunk?
5. I went to a dance there once.
6. It is good sense not to take chances.
7. I rinse my hair with hot water.
8. Jill has danced since she was six.
9. They plunge into the river to swim.
10. That does not make sense to me.
11. I danced with a prince once.
12. She looks like she is in a trance.
13. A red fence hid the trash cans.
14. I get tense when the kids yell.
15. Once I had a chance to marry Pat.
16. Ann put a fringe on her skirt.

102

Note: To read the letters -ng, you do not say /n/ and then add /g/.
The letters -ng together make one sound: /ng/.

Practice 32: -ng

1. **-ng**

win	ban
wing	bang

2. What does the word end with?

         n   **g**   **ng**

1. ra**g**
2. spri**ng**
3. ba**ng**
4. wi**g**
5. ru**n**
6. ga**ng**
7. si**ng**
8. fa**n**

9. bri**ng**
10. sa**g**
11. lu**ng**
12. pa**n**
13. ta**g**
14. su**n**
15. thi**n**
16. hu**g**

3. Write the letters and say the word.

      ng   **ng**

ba **ng**	bri **ng**
ga **ng**	sli **ng**
ha **ng**	sti **ng**
ki **ng**	swi **ng**
ri **ng**	spri **ng**
si **ng**	stri **ng**
wi **ng**	hu **ng**
thi **ng**	lu **ng**

4. Read the words.

ring	sing
thing	swing
sting	spring
king	lung
sling	hung
bring	gang
wing	bang
string	hang

5. Write the word you hear.

1. _wing_
2. _sting_
3. _hang_
4. _sling_
5. _lung_
6. _bring_
7. _string_
8. _gang_

9. _sing_
10. _king_
11. _thing_
12. _spring_
13. _bang_
14. _hung_
15. _swing_
16. _ring_

6. Read the sentences.
New word: something
Review word: finger

1. The ring does not fit my finger.
2. Bob hangs out with a street gang.
3. I think something is stinging me!
4. Andy hung up the telephone.
5. The doctor put Ed's arm in a sling.
6. Bring me something to put on.
7. He has a big string of fish.
8. Jack will sing at the spring dance.
9. The king asks for something to drink.
10. Scott bangs on his drums.
11. They fix the wing of the jet.
12. We stop work when the bell rings.
13. A gang of kids plays on the swings.
14. Smog hurts your lungs.
15. The picture is hanging by a string.
16. The King Family sings on TV.

Practice 33: -nk

1. **-nk**

wing   bang

wink   bank

2. What does the word end with?

     n   k   nk

1. ba**nk**
2. ra**n**
3. duc**k**
4. li**nk**
5. stic**k**
6. si**n**
7. tac**k**
8. bu**n**
9. pi**nk**
10. sti**nk**
11. wi**n**
12. stu**n**
13. cra**nk**
14. tru**nk**
15. bri**nk**
16. thic**k**

3. Write the letters and say the word.

    n k   **n k**

ba **nk**   wi **nk**

ra **nk**   thi **nk**

ta **nk**   dri **nk**

ya **nk**   sti **nk**

li **nk**   shri **nk**

pi **nk**   bu **nk**

ri **nk**   du **nk**

si **nk**   ju **nk**

4. Read the words.

wink	drink
pink	dunk
stink	junk
think	bunk
link	yank
sink	rank
rink	bank
shrink	tank

5. Write the word you hear.

1. _yank_   9. _wink_
2. _sink_   10. _junk_
3. _dunk_   11. _tank_
4. _link_   12. _drink_
5. _stink_   13. _bunk_
6. _pink_   14. _shrink_
7. _bank_   15. _rank_
8. _rink_   16. _think_

6. Read the sentences.
   Review words: past, thank, Frank, Hank

1. I think we have money in the bank.
2. Frank winks at Peg.
3. Do not dunk that pot in water.
4. He ranks number one in my class.
5. Thanks for giving us the bunk beds.
6. I think that is funny!
7. Put this junk in the trash can.
8. Hank drinks a glass of water.
9. The fish sinks in the tank.
10. She fell down at the rink.
11. Fill out this pink slip.
12. My pants will shrink if they get wet.
13. This trash stinks!
14. He yanks the paper out of my hands.
15. Grandmother is my link with the past.
16. Thanks for filling up the gas tank.

104

Practice 34: More Practice with -ng and -nk

T. says: Now you have studied many words that end with *n-g* and *n-k*. This practice will give you help in telling the sounds apart. It will also introduce you to many *n-g* and *n-k* words you haven't had before.

1

T. says: Let's practice the sounds first. (Point to *-ng*.)

Remember that *n-g* makes the sound /ng/.

Say the sound /ng/. [S: /ng/] Good. (Point to *nk*.)

And *n-k* is made up of the sound /ng/, plus the sound /k/.

So *n-k* sounds like /nk/. Say /nk/. [S: /nk/] Good.

These pairs of words will help you tell the sounds apart.

(Point to *wing*.) What is this word? [S: wing] Good.

(Point to *wink*.) And this one? [S: wink] Yes.

Can you hear the difference in the ending sounds?

Help S. if he has trouble. Repeat this process for *bang* and *bank* and *sung* and *sunk*.

What does the word end with?

T. says: Now I will read some words. You listen for the ending sounds.

If the word ends with the *n-g* sound /ng/, write *n-g* in the blank.

If it ends with the *n-k* sounds /nk/, write *n-k* in the blank.

Go through the first few words with S. to make sure he knows what to do. If S. repeats the words after you, make sure he pronounces them correctly. You may want to correct S.'s mistakes in this part before going on to part 2. You can correct them as he makes them, or at the end of the part.

2

T. says: Now you will learn many *n-g* words and *n-k* words that are similar to the ones you already know. Only the vowels are different. Look at the chart of words below. (Point to chart.) These words describe *actions*—they tell about things that are *happening*.

This first column of words (point to first column) tells about things that are happening in the *present* time (point to explanation at top of part 2).

These words are used to tell about things that happen now or happen again and again.

For example: "I *sing* every day."

The second column (point to second column) tells about things that have happened, that are finished, or *past* (point to the explanation).

For example: "I *sang* yesterday."

T. says: Sometimes you need a third word if you are using *has* or *have* (point to third column). For example: "I have *sung* since I was ten. "

(Point to the explanation.)

You are using the word *have*, so you must use *sung* after it.

All of those words—*sing, sang,* and *sung*—tell about the same kind of action. But *sing* is used for the present time, *sang* is used for the past time, and *sung* is used after *has* and *have*.

Let's look at other words that go together like *sing, sang,* and *sung.*

Only the vowels are different in the words.

Go through the list of words, encouraging S. to sound out the words himself. Talk about what the words mean, and use them in sentences with the words *now, again and again, yesterday,* and *has* and *have*. Point out that for the last six words on the list, the past form is the same as the word to be used after *has* and *have*. Encourage S. to make up his own sentences with the words.

3 Use the *past* of the word.

T. says: Now you have learned the *past* of some common words.

Look at each word that comes before the sentences.

Write the past form of that word in the blank. Then read the sentence.

Help S. if he needs it, letting him refer to the chart in part 2 if he forgets the words. Check S.'s work.

Use the word that goes with *has* or *have*.

T. says: Now look at the word that comes before the sentences.

In the blank, write the form of that word that goes with *have* or *has*.

Then read the sentence.

Help S. if he needs it. Check his work.

136

Practice 34: More Practice with -ng and -nk

1. **-ng** wing bang sung
   -nk wink bank sunk

What does the word end with?

	ng	nk

1. cli**ng**
2. ta**ng**
3. ho**nk**
4. ra**nk**
5. su**ng**
6. ki**ng**
7. bla**nk**
8. ha**ng**
9. bri**nk**
10. stro**ng**
11. stu**nk**
12. you**ng**
13. sa**nk**
14. sli**ng**
15. wi**nk**
16. ga**ng**
17. lu**ng**
18. thi**nk**
19. chu**nk**
20. spri**ng**
21. wro**ng**
22. sti**nk**
23. cla**ng**
24. tru**nk**
25. fla**nk**
26. si**ng**
27. flu**ng**
28. ya**nk**
29. ri**nk**
30. hu**nk**
31. ba**ng**
32. pi**nk**

2. The **present** is used for things that happen again and again.

   I **sing** every day.

The **past** is used for things that happened and are finished.

   I **sang** yesterday.

And some forms of these words are used with **has** or **have**.

   I **have sung** since I was ten.

Every day	Yesterday	has/have +
ring	rang	rung
sing	sang	sung
spring	sprang	sprung
drink	drank	drunk
sink	sank	sunk
stink	stank	stunk
shrink	shrank	shrunk

Every day	Yesterday	has/have +
cling	clung	clung
fling	flung	flung
sting	stung	stung
string	strung	strung
swing	swung	swung
hang	hung	hung

3. Use the **past** of the word.

sink   1. The ship **sank** yesterday.

hang   2. We **hung** up the picture.

fling   3. She **flung** her bag down.

ring   4. My telephone **rang**.

string   5. They **strung** up the net.

cling   6. Jimmy **clung** to my hand.

drink   7. The baby **drank** from a cup.

spring   8. Dad **sprang** out of bed.

Use the word that goes with **has** or **have**.

ring   1. The bell for class has **rung**.

hang   2. He has **hung** up his shirt.

sing   3. We have **sung** at dances.

shrink   4. The dresses have **shrunk**.

drink   5. Jim has **drunk** some water.

stink   6. The trash has **stunk** for days.

swing   7. Bob has **swung** the bat.

sting   8. No bugs have **stung** us.

105

Practice 35: Review of Ending *n* Blends

1 **Look at the picture and say the word.**
Then write the letters of the ending blend you hear.

T. says: What is this? (Point to picture.) [S: wink]

The ending blend is missing in the word.

What sounds does *wink* end with? [S: /nk/]
Good.

What letters make the sounds /nk/? Write the letters in the blank.

For the word *king,* ask about the *sound* it ends with rather than the *sounds,* since the letters *-ng* together make one sound, /ng/.

For the word *fence,* ask "What letters make the sounds /ns/ in *fence*?"

Check S.'s work. As you go over each of the words, make sure S. gives the correct pronunciation.

2 **Practice the blends you have learned. Make at least 12 words with these beginnings and endings.**

T. says: Now you will make some blend words.

In this column are some ending *n* blends that you have studied. (Point to second column.)

And in this column are beginnings of words. (Point to first column.)

Put the word beginnings together with the ending blends to make real words. The words will be ones you've seen before.

Make as many words as you can. Try to make at least 12 words.

Write the words on the lines at right.

Help S. as he makes the words. S. may want to take one ending blend at a time, matching it with each beginning to make possible words.

3 **Fill in the blends to make sense in the sentences.**

T. says: Here are some sentences to read. But parts of some of the words are missing. There is a space for each blend that is missing.

You must fill in the right *n* blend to make words that will make sense in the sentence.

S. may immediately recognize the blend necessary to make the word that fits. Or S. may read the sentence, leaving out the word to be filled in, and try to think of the word. If S. cannot guess the word from reading the sentence, he may want to try the *n* blends one by one, to see if they make words and, if so, if the words fit. After S. fills in the correct blend, you may want him to read the sentence again.

You may want to refer to Appendixes D-F for ideas on adding endings to the words S. has learned.

138

Practice 35: Review of Ending n Blends: -nt, -nd, -nch, -nge, -nce, -nse, -ng, -nk

1. Look at the picture and say the word. Then write the letters of the ending blend you hear.

1.

wi _nk_

4.

ki _ng_

2.

a _nt_

5.

ba _nd_

3.

be _nch_

6.

fe _nce_

2. Practice the blends you have learned.

Make at least 12 words with these beginnings and endings.

pu	nd	bench	punk
wi	nt	bend	punt
ra	nch	bent	ranch
be	ng	hunch	rang
hu	nk	hung	rank
		hunk	wind
		punch	wing

3. Fill in the blends to make sense in the sentences.

nk nt nch nce nse nd nge ng

1. Andy's aunt went out to lu_nch_ and spent twenty dollars.

2. This bunch of numbers makes no se_nse_ to me.

3. She has tended the pla_nt_s since spring.

4. The ga_ng_ hangs out at the ranch every cha_nce_ they get.

5. Tha_nk_ you for bringing me some punch to dri_nk_.

6. The blo_nd_ girl can sing and da_nce_.

7. I think I will take a plu_nge_ in the river.

8. Give me a ha_nd_. I will pitch this tent on the sa_nd_.

9. The pi_nk_ pants are covered with li_nt_.

10. I spe_nt_ the funds. But the bank can le_nd_ me money.

106

Other Ending Blends

For the remaining blends practices, follow the same procedures as for the previous ending blends, except for part 1 of 37-A, 37-B, 41, and 42, and part 2 of 37-B.

Follow this procedure for part 1 of these exercises. This one is for Practice 37-A.

1

T. says: This word is *fat*. (Point to first word.) Read *fat*. [S: fat] Good.

Fat ends with the letter *t*, so the last sound is /t/.

And this word is *fast*. (Point to *fast*.) Read *fast*. [S: fast]

The word *fast* is just like *fat*, except it has an *s* before the *t*.

The letter *s* makes the sound /s/, and *t* makes the sound /t/, and when they come together at the end, you blend the sounds together to sound like /st/.

Say the blend /st/. [S: /st/] Good.

What is this word? (Point to first word.) [S: fat]

And this word? (Point to second word.) [S: fast]

Can you hear the extra *s* sound in *fast*?

Can you hear the *s-t* making the blend /st/ at the end of the word?

(Help S. with the words again if he has trouble. Go over the other examples.)

This is for Practice 37-B.

2 Circle the word you hear

Part 2 of these practices is designed to help S. discriminate between frequently confused ending sounds.

Follow this procedure.

T. says: You have been studying the ending blend *s-t*.

The *s-t* blend is often confused with *t-s* at the end of words.

This exercise will help you tell the difference.

I will read some words. Listen for the sounds at the end of each word.

If it sounds like the word has the *s-t* blend /st/ at the end, circle the word on the right.

If it sounds like the word ends with *t-s*, /ts/, circle the word on the left. Ready? *Nets. Nets.*

Read each word slowly at least twice. It may help S. to repeat the words after you. If he does, make sure he pronounces each one correctly. If S. has trouble with the first word, contrast *nets* with *nest*, explaining the difference.

If S. has much difficulty with this part, he may need more exercises like this one to practice. As there is a very limited number of actual words that can be contrasted in this way, you may have to use nonsense words. This confusion of the *s* sounds at the end is common with the ending blends *-st, -sk,* and *-sp.* If you would like to give S. practice with *-sk* and *-sp,* give him this exercise:

Circle the word you hear.

1.	backs	bask
2.	decks	desk
3.	bricks	brisk
4.	tacks	task
5.	ducks	dusk
6.	gaps	gasp
7.	lips	lisp
8.	claps	clasp

140

Practice 36: -mp

1. **-mp**

dam	bum
damp	bump

2. What does the word end with?

    m   **p**   **mp**

1. da**mp**
2. swa**p**
3. shri**mp**
4. cla**m**
5. lu**mp**
6. cha**p**
7. plu**m**
8. pu**p**
9. stu**mp**
10. hu**m**
11. la**p**
12. thu**mp**
13. ski**mp**
14. slu**m**
15. tra**p**
16. ra**m**

3. Write the letters and say the word.

	mp		**mp**
ca	_mp_	li	_mp_
da	_mp_	shri	_mp_
la	_mp_	bu	_mp_
ra	_mp_	du	_mp_
cha	_mp_	lu	_mp_
cra	_mp_	plu	_mp_
tra	_mp_	stu	_mp_
sta	_mp_	pu	_mp_

4. Read the words.

lump	ramp
stump	camp
pump	stamp
dump	lamp
bump	tramp
plump	damp
shrimp	champ
limp	cramp

5. Write the word you hear.

1. _dump_
2. _lamp_
3. _stamp_
4. _pump_
5. _camp_
6. _ramp_
7. _limp_
8. _stump_
9. _champ_
10. _tramp_
11. _lump_
12. _damp_
13. _cramp_
14. _shrimp_
15. _plump_
16. _bump_

6. Read the sentences.
Review word: jump

1. At camp, we get water from a pump.
2. Take that lamp to the dump.
3. Don has a cramp in his leg.
   It makes him limp.
4. This letter has no stamp on it.
5. Tom bumped his head and got a big lump.
6. Ned dumps the shrimp in a pan.
7. I jump in my car and head for our camp.
8. I will dig up the stump in my yard.
9. We hung up the damp shirts.
10. There are bumps in our street.
11. Jim is plump. He wants to be thin.
12. Rub the lamp with a damp rag.
13. We look like tramps.
14. He is the winner and still champ!
15. The car got on the ramp.

107

Note: Point out that *guest* is spelled with a *u*.
    Instructions for part 1 are on page 140.

Practice 37-A: -st

1.   -st

fat   pet

fast   pest

2. What does the word end with?

            s   t   st

1. ju**st**   9. mis**s**
2. pas**s**   10. ve**t**
3. li**t**   11. la**st**
4. mi**st**   12. gues**s**
5. we**t**   13. cru**st**
6. les**s**   14. pe**st**
7. ca**st**   15. los**s**
8. ru**t**   16. pa**t**

3. Write the letters and say the word.

        st   st

ca __st__   gue __st__
fa __st__   ne __st__
la __st__   pe __st__
ma __st__   re __st__
pa __st__   te __st__
va __st__   ve __st__
bla __st__   we __st__
be __st__   che __st__

4. Read the words.

    test   pest
    nest   last
    chest   cast
    guest   mast
    vest   blast
    best   fast
    west   vast
    rest   past

5. Write the word you hear.

1. __west__   9. __guest__
2. __last__   10. __fast__
3. __rest__   11. __test__
4. __cast__   12. __blast__
5. __chest__   13. __vest__
6. __vast__   14. __mast__
7. __best__   15. __pest__
8. __past__   16. __nest__

6. Read the sentences.
New word: day
Review word: left

1. The car is headed west, going fast.
2. The bird builds a nest out of twigs.
3. Do your best on the rest of the test.
4. Dr. King put my leg in a cast.
5. The last guest left at half past ten.
6. This brand of pest killer is the best.
7. Ted ran fast. He ran past the shop.
8. Dan's ranch out west is vast.
9. He will test that car last.
10. Put this red vest in the chest.
11. The ship has a big mast.
12. No one was hurt in the blast.
13. I will fast for the rest of the day.
14. Our guest wants to rest.
15. Ed's chest hurts.
    Dr. Bell tells him to rest.

108

142

Practice 37-B: -st

1. -st

lit   rut

list   rust

2. Circle the word you hear.

1. (nets)   nest
2. fits   (fist)
3. vets   (vest)
4. ruts   (rust)
5. (bets)   best
6. (pats)   past
7. (cats)   cast
8. wets   (west)

3. Write the letters and say the word.

	st		st
fi	st	gu	st
li	st	ju	st
mi	st	mu	st
twi	st	ru	st
bu	st	cru	st
du	st	tru	st

4. Read the words.

just   mist

rust   fist

bust   twist

must   list

trust

gust

crust

dust

5. Write the word you hear.

1. must   7. fist
2. gust   8. dust
3. rust   9. twist
4. list   10. crust
5. just   11. mist
6. trust   12. bust

6. Read the sentences.
New word: off
Review word: sister

1. Cut the crusts off the bread.
2. Dusting is the last job on my list.
3. My car has just started to rust.
4. This thread is twisted.
5. You must have trust in your friends.
6. He punched the bag with his fists.
7. A gust of wind carried off my hat.
8. There is just one test I must take.
9. A thick mist covered the pond.
10. Mr. Hill set up a trust fund.
11. I must make out a shopping list.
12. Put the apple filling into the crust.
13. My sister just dusted off the chest.
14. The pot was covered with rust.
15. You can trust that judge to be just.
16. Dan twisted the lid off the jar.

109

Practice 38: -sk, -sp

1.

-sk	-sp
mass	gas
mask	gasp

2. What does the word end with?

s k sk
1. tuc_k_
2. du_sk_
3. mas_s_
4. bric_k_
5. fla_sk_
6. dec_k_
7. ri_sk_
8. bas_s_

s p sp
1. clas_s_
2. whi_p_
3. cri_sp_
4. li_p_
5. ga_s_
6. wa_sp_
7. cla_p_
8. gra_sp_

3. Write the letters and say the word.

sk	**sk**	**sp**
a _sk_	du _sk_	ga _sp_
ma _sk_	hu _sk_	cla _sp_
ta _sk_	tu _sk_	gra _sp_
de _sk_		cri _sp_
ri _sk_		
whi _sk_		
bri _sk_		

4. Read the words.

desk	brisk	crisp
husk	whisk	gasp
tusk	mask	grasp
dusk	ask	clasp
risk	task	

5. Write the word you hear.

1. _risk_
2. _ask_
3. _tusk_
4. _clasp_
5. _desk_
6. _husk_
7. _task_
8. _gasp_
9. _whisk_
10. _crisp_
11. _mask_
12. _brisk_
13. _grasp_
14. _dusk_

6. Read the sentences.
New word: boy
Review words: corn, basket

1. The farmer worked until dusk.
2. Tom asked if there was a big risk.
3. The boys and girls sit at their desks.
4. The cab whisked him off to his office.
5. This is a list of tasks for you to do.
6. My little boy has a funny mask.
7. I was gasping after I ran up the steps.
8. I step out into the crisp, brisk wind.
9. Her task was to cut the grass.
10. Put the corn husks into the basket.
11. You take a risk when you bet money.
12. That boy put on his catcher's mask.
13. This bread has a crisp crust.
14. She grasped my hand and clasped it.
15. Ed asks if he can work at her desk.
16. The pig has two big tusks.

110

Note: Point out that the *u* is silent in *guilt, built,* and *build.*
Point out the difference in spelling and meaning between *build* and *built.*

Practice 39: -lt, -ld

1.

-lt	-ld
bell	well
belt	weld

2. What does the word end with?

	l t lt		l d ld
1.	bell	1.	weld
2.	colt	2.	feel
3.	till	3.	head
4.	bit	4.	mill
5.	melt	5.	mild
6.	bowl	6.	told
7.	wilt	7.	bill
8.	tot	8.	gold

3. Write the letters and say the word.

	lt		ld
be	lt	he	ld
fe	lt	we	ld
me	lt	bui	ld
bui	lt		
gui	lt		
qui	lt		
ti	lt		
wi	lt		

4. Read the words.

tilt	build
built	weld
wilt	held
quilt	
guilt	
melt	
belt	
felt	

5. Write the word you hear.

1. wilt
2. felt
3. held
4. built
5. tilt
6. belt
7. quilt
8. weld
9. guilt
10. melt
11. build

6. Read the sentences.
New words: over, together
Review word: butter

1. Grandmother is making a quilt.
2. The belt held up his pants.
3. Melt the fat in the pan.
4. Dad built a desk. It held together.
5. The robber cannot get rid of his guilt.
6. My plant is wilting.
7. We worked together to build the school.
8. When he tilted it back, it fell over.
9. Andy welds two things together.
10. Dan plans to build six buildings.
11. The belt felt good when I put it on.
12. Put the quilt over the bed.
13. Mom held her baby. The baby felt wet.
14. They built a bridge over the river.
15. She felt guilt over what happened.
16. Put the melted butter on the corn.

111

Note: Point out that *self* can be used alone or in compound words like
herself, himself, myself, yourself, and *itself.*

Practice 40: -lk, -lf, -lp, -lm

1.

-lk	**-lf**	**-lp**	**-lm**
mill	shell	hell	fill
milk	shelf	help	film

2. What does the word end with?

l k lk		l f lf
1. bil**l**		1. i**f**
2. e**lk**		2. go**lf**
3. sic**k**		3. woo**l**
4. mi**lk**		4. e**lf**
5. buc**k**		5. sel**l**
6. wel**l**		6. snif**f**
7. su**lk**		7. gul**l**
8. hul**l**		8. she**lf**

3. Write the letters and say the word.

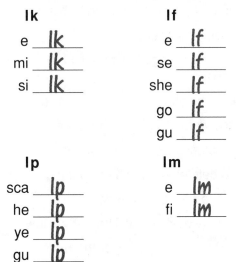

lk		**lf**
e ___**lk**___		e ___**lf**___
mi ___**lk**___		se ___**lf**___
si ___**lk**___		she ___**lf**___
		go ___**lf**___
		gu ___**lf**___

lp		**lm**
sca ___**lp**___		e ___**lm**___
he ___**lp**___		fi ___**lm**___
ye ___**lp**___		
gu ___**lp**___		

4. Read the words.

silk	help	golf	film
milk	yelp	self	elm
elk	gulp	shelf	
	scalp	elf	
		gulf	

5. Write the word you hear.

1. _help_	8. _milk_
2. _gulf_	9. _elm_
3. _film_	10. _scalp_
4. _silk_	11. _golf_
5. _elf_	12. _yelp_
6. _gulp_	13. _self_
7. _shelf_	14. _elk_

6. Read the sentences.

1. I am making a silk dress for myself.
2. The ship headed into the gulf.
3. I take colored pictures with this film.
4. Pam gulped down a glass of milk.
5. Stan plays golf by himself.
6. We helped Dad cut down the big elm.
7. Scott will put up the shelf himself.
8. The baby wants to do things for herself.
9. My uncle is in the Elks Club.
10. Frank helps himself to some milk.
11. The little elf had fun playing tricks.
12. The silk thread is on the top shelf.
13. She helped me when I hurt myself.
14. The class is watching a good film.
15. The pup yelps when it is hurt.
16. This hat makes my scalp itch!

112

Practice 41: -ft

1.   -ft

rat   sit

raft   sift

2. What does the word end with?

f   t   ft

1. dea**f**
2. ra**ft**
3. si**t**
4. the**ft**
5. ca**t**
6. of**f**
7. li**ft**
8. hal**f**
9. le**t**
10. shi**ft**
11. a**t**
12. cle**f**
13. gi**ft**
14. sough**t**
15. dra**ft**
16. puf**f**

3. Write the letters and say the word.

ft   ft

ra **ft**   li **ft**

sha **ft**   si **ft**

cra **ft**   shi **ft**

dra **ft**   thri **ft**

le **ft**   dri **ft**

the **ft**   swi **ft**

gi **ft**

4. Read the words.

sift	craft
drift	raft
shift	shaft
swift	draft
thrift	theft
gift	left
lift	

5. Write the word you hear.

1. _gift_
2. _craft_
3. _drift_
4. _swift_
5. _left_
6. _raft_
7. _sift_
8. _thrift_
9. _draft_
10. _shift_
11. _theft_
12. _lift_
13. _shaft_

6. Read the sentences.
New word: after

1. The raft drifted down the river.
2. Sift it to get the lumps out.
3. That draft is giving me a chill.
4. Kim cannot lift her arm.
5. I stress thrift. I do not spend much.
6. I had no money left to pay for the gift.
7. That man is wanted for car theft.
8. We work the last shift at the factory.
9. We asked him for a lift into the city.
10. After one, I left for my crafts class.
11. My aunt works with gifted children.
12. Jack drifted from one job to another.
13. Jill's car has a stick shift.
14. Ned is a swift runner.
15. He tripped and fell down the dark shaft.
16. Ron is skilled in his craft.

113

Practice 42: -pt, -ct, -xt

1.

-pt	-ct	-xt
wet	fat	net
wept	fact	next

2. What does the word end with?

p   t   pt

1. wra*p*
2. ke*pt*
3. swea*t*
4. fli*p*
5. we*pt*
6. cro*p*
7. a*t*
8. scri*pt*

c   t   ct

1. ele*ct*
2. die*t*
3. rea*ct*
4. basi*c*
5. pilo*t*
6. atti*c*
7. dedu*ct*
8. magi*c*

3. Write the letters and say the word.

pt	**ct**	**xt**
a _*pt*_	a _*ct*_	ne _*xt*_
ke _*pt*_	fa _*ct*_	te _*xt*_
we _*pt*_	stri _*ct*_	
cre _*pt*_		
sle _*pt*_		
swe _*pt*_		
scri _*pt*_		

4. Read the words.

crept	fact	text
wept	act	next
slept	strict	
kept		
swept		
script		
apt		

5. Write the word you hear.

1. *swept*
2. *act*
3. *script*
4. *wept*
5. *text*
6. *apt*
7. *fact*
8. *slept*
9. *next*
10. *kept*
11. *strict*
12. *crept*

6. Read the sentences.
New words: study, adopt, expect
Review words: factory, doctor

1. The judge will study the facts.
2. We kept expecting something to happen.
3. We want to adopt our next kid.
4. Dad acted fast. He swept up the glass.
5. The doctor has not slept much for days.
6. The crab crept over the sand.
7. I expect Ed will act in our next play. He is studying the script for it.
8. We expect to adopt her plan.
9. This is the next text we will study.
10. Pam felt so sad that she wept.
11. The baby crept into the kitchen.
12. He is apt to be strict if they act up.
13. The pup slept next to my bed.
14. This text gives facts on adopted kids.
15. John kept his job at the factory.

114

Practice 43: Review of Other Ending Blends: -mp, -st, -sk, -sp, -lk, -lf, -lm, -lp, -ct, -pt, -xt

1. Look at the picture and say the word. Then write the letters of the ending blend you hear.

1.

mi __lk__

3.

de __sk__

5.

gi __ft__

2.

pu __mp__

4.

ve __st__

6.

be __lt__

2. Circle all the words that are the same as the first one.

mask	mash	(mask)	ask	mast	mash	smack	(mask)
left	lift	felt	(left)	let	(left)	slept	(left)
past	(past)	pat	(past)	pest	pact	(past)	spat
belt	bet	(belt)	bell	built	pelt	(belt)	(belt)

3. Draw a line from each beginning to an ending blend to make a word.

mi ⟍   xt
fa   ft
ne   ct
dra   lk

tu   sp
cri   sk
sta   pt
we   mp

4. Use these words to fill in the blanks:

shelf   held   film   help   list   guilt   west   risks

1. The car left the camp, heading **west** on the ramp.

2. Dust the **shelf** and put the lamp on it.

3. My guest asked me if I wanted any **help** .

4. The fact was, he felt no **guilt** for his acts.

5. The champ kept taking **risks**.

6. Make a **list** of the tasks you do best.

7. I **held** the golf club and lifted it over my head.

8. Andy gasped when he watched the **film** .

115

Vowels + r

The next nine practices cover the most common sounds of the r-controlled vowels *er, ir, ur, ar,* and *or.* The procedure is the same as for the blends practices except for parts 1 and 2.

1

The first part of each practice gives words that have the r-controlled vowel sound S. is studying. Follow this procedure, as with *er*:

T. says: When you have an *r* after any of the vowels, it usually changes the sound of the vowel.
The vowel doesn't have a regular short sound.
E-r sounds like /er/ not /ehr/.
What does *e-r* sound like? [/er/] Good.
Here are some words that have the *e-r* sound /er/.

Go over each word, helping S. if he has trouble. Some words may be new to him.

As you do part 1 for the first three practices, remind S.:

T. says: *E-r, i-r,* and *u-r* all make the same sound. They sound like /er/.
You will have to remember whether the /er/ sound in words is spelled with *e-r, i-r,* or *u-r,* because you can't tell how the word is spelled by the sound of it.

2 Write the letters you hear.

This exercise helps S. distinguish between the *vowel-r* combination he is studying, and the reverse, the *r-vowel* combination. Follow this procedure:

T. says: You have been studying the *e-r* sound /er/.
It is easy to confuse the *e-r* sound /ur/ with the *r-e* sound /re/ in words, especially when you are spelling them.
This exercise will help you tell the difference.
I will read some words.
If it sounds like the word has the *e-r* sound /er/, write *e-r* in the blank.
If it sounds like the word has the *r-e* sound /re/, write *r-e* in the blank.
Ready? *Term. Term.*

Read each word slowly and distinctly, at least twice. If S. repeats the words after you, make sure he pronounces each one correctly. As he does the exercise, S. might first see if he can recognize the *vowel-r* sound he has been studying. If S. has trouble with a word, you might contrast the word with the word as it would be with the reverse sound (even if that word is a nonsense word). If S. has much difficulty with this part, he may need more exercises like this one to practice.

3 Write the letters and say the word.

In this part, S. will be blending the r-controlled vowel with consonants and consonant digraphs at the beginning and ending to make words. The words are grouped together by ending sounds.

T. says: What does *e-r* sound like? (Point to *er* at top of column.) [S: /er/]
Good. You can make new words that have the /er/ sound in them.
(Point to *h*.) *H* sounds like /h/. Say /h/. [S: /h/]
If I write *e-r* after *h* (write the letters in), I have the sounds /h/ and /er/. Say those sounds as I point to them.
(Point to *h*.) [S: /h/] (Point to *er*.) [S: /er/] Good.
Can you blend those sounds together into a word?
(Help S. if he has trouble.) [S: her] Right.
(Point to *v*.) *V* sounds like /v/. Say /v/. [S: /v/]
And *b* sounds like /b/. Say /b/. [S: /b/] Good.
If I have *v* and then *e-r* (write letters in), and then *b*, I have the sounds /v/ and /er/ and /b/. Say those sounds as I point to them.
(Point to *v*.) [S: /v/] (Point to *er*.) [S: /er/] (Point to *b*.) [S: /b/]
Good. Can you blend those sounds together into a word?
(Help S. if he has trouble.) [S: verb] Right.
Now let's go through the rest of the words.
All the words have the sound /er/, spelled with *e-r*.
You write the letters and read the words.

For the rest of the practice, follow the same procedure as for the other blends practices.

In practices 47-A, 47-B, and 47-C make sure S. pronounces the *ar* sound /ar/ correctly. Be sure S. distinguishes it from the /ur/ sound. See page 157 for a discussion of the *or* sound.

150

Practice 44: er

1.   er

her	were
fern	jerk

2. Write the letters you hear.

	er	**re**
1. t _er_ m		5. _re_ d
2. f _re_ t		6. d _re_ ss
3. v _er_ b		7. cl _er_ k
4. f _er_ n		8. f _re_ sh

3. Write the letters and say the word.

er	**er**
h _er_	f _er_ n
v _er_ b	F _er_ n
h _er_ d	st _er_ n
m _er_ ge	v _er_ se
j _er_ k	n _er_ ve
p _er_ k	s _er_ ve
cl _er_ k	sw _er_ ve
t _er_ m	p _er_ ch

4. Read the words.

term	serve
Fern	nerve
fern	swerve
stern	herd
her	perch
perk	verb
jerk	merge
clerk	verse

5. Write the word you hear.

1. _jerk_	9. _stern_
2. _serve_	10. _verb_
3. _fern_	11. _merge_
4. _perch_	12. _Fern_
5. _term_	13. _clerk_
6. _her_	14. _verse_
7. _nerve_	15. _swerve_
8. _perk_	16. _herd_

6. Read the sentences.
Review words: were, heard, person

1. Fern pays the clerk in the gift shop.
2. I heard him sing the last verse.
3. Make a list of the helping verbs.
4. They serve fresh perch for lunch.
5. Dan is a very strict and stern person.
6. The van stopped with a jerk.
7. I have just one term paper to write.
8. Pam likes ferns best of any plants.
9. The cars merge when they get off the ramp.
10. A hot drink will perk you up.
11. We heard her yelling at the clerk.
    She has a lot of nerve!
12. The car had to swerve to miss the pup.
13. The bird is resting on the perch.
14. Don will serve two terms in office.
15. We were herding the pigs into the pen.

116

Practice 45: ir

1. **ir**

bird

girl

skirt

2. Write the letters you hear.

	ir	ri		
1. t __ri__ m		5. f __ir__ st
2. d __ir__ t		6. g __ri__ ll
3. b __ir__ ch		7. t __ri__ p
4. c __ri__ b		8. f __ir__ m

3. Write the letters and say the word.

ir	ir
f __ir__	ch __ir__ p
s __ir__	d __ir__ t
st __ir__	sh __ir__ t
th __ir__ d	squ __ir__ t
wh __ir__ l	b __ir__ ch
tw __ir__ l	b __ir__ th
f __ir__ m	f __ir__ st
squ __ir__ m	th __ir__ st

4. Read the words.

firm	sir
squirm	stir
shirt	fir
dirt	birth
squirt	thirst
twirl	first
whirl	third
chirp	birch

5. Write the word you hear.

1. shirt	9. sir
2. twirl	10. birth
3. fir	11. whirl
4. birch	12. squirm
5. chirp	13. third
6. firm	14. dirt
7. squirt	15. first
8. thirst	16. stir

6. Read the sentences.
New word: tree
Review words: bird, girl, skirt

1. Stir in the eggs first, then the nuts.
2. I got dirt on my shirt and my skirt.
3. We planted birch trees and fir trees.
4. I was thrilled after my son's birth!
5. Dad is firm when he says no.
6. The bird sits in the tree, chirping.
7. You will be first, and I will be third.
8. Pat whirls and twirls when she dances.
9. The little girl sat and squirmed.
10. This drink will quench your thirst.
11. Stir it until it gets firm.
12. The pup got mud and dirt on Ed's shirt.
13. Ed says "Yes, sir" to his father.
14. She is giving birth to her third baby.
15. Fern has on a pink skirt.
16. He squirts water on the thirsty plants.

117

152

Practice 46: ur

1. **ur**

    hurt

    burn

    nurse

2. Write the letters you hear.

        ur   **ru**

1. c _ur_ l   5. g _ru_ ff
2. d _ru_ g   6. c _ru_ sh
3. b _ur_ p   7. c _ur_ b
4. t _ur_ n   8. d _ru_ m

3. Write the letters and say the word.

     ur   **ur**

f _ur_   ch _ur_ n

p _ur_ r   b _ur_ p

bl _ur_   c _ur_ se

c _ur_ b   n _ur_ se

s _ur_ f   p _ur_ se

_ur_ ge   c _ur_ ve

c _ur_ l   ch _ur_ ch

t _ur_ n   b _ur_ st

4. Read the words.

curl	curb
churn	purr
turn	fur
purse	blur
curse	church
nurse	burst
surf	curve
urge	burp

5. Write the word you hear.

1. _nurse_   9. _fur_
2. _purr_   10. _burst_
3. _surf_   11. _curve_
4. _burp_   12. _purse_
5. _urge_   13. _church_
6. _curb_   14. _turn_
7. _curse_   15. _blur_
8. _churn_   16. _curl_

6. Read the sentences.
New word: wife
Review words: hurt, burn, hurry, curtains, cover

1. My cat purrs when I rub her fur.
2. The car turns and stops at the curb.
3. A man grabbed my purse and hurried off.
4. One person is hurt. His hand is burned.

    A nurse covers the burns on his hand.
5. We sit in the sand and watch the surf.
6. Ted's wife urges him to go to church.
7. She fills up her purse. It is bursting!
8. The farmer's wife churns the butter.
9. Fran is curling her hair.
10. Bill burst into the church office.
11. Jim cursed when he hurt his finger.
12. Hurry up and put up the curtains!
13. My wife is burping our baby.
14. The nurses take turns working.
15. The car went fast on the curve.

118

Note: The word *mark* is used as both a common and proper noun.

Practice 47-A: ar

1. ar

car   mark
barn   park

2. Write the letters you hear.

ra	ar
1. d _ar_ k	5. d _ra_ g
2. g _ra_ b	6. sh _ar_ p
3. b _ar_ n	7. c _ra_ sh
4. _ra_ t	8. p _ar_ k

3. Write the letters and say the word.

ar	ar
b _ar_	b _ar_ k
c _ar_	d _ar_ k
f _ar_	l _ar_ k
j _ar_	m _ar_ k
t _ar_	M _ar_ k
sc _ar_	p _ar_ k
st _ar_	sh _ar_ k
y _ar_ n	sp _ar_ k

4. Read the words.

park	yarn
Mark	far
bark	tar
shark	car
dark	jar
spark	star
mark	bar
lark	scar

5. Write the word you hear.

1. _lark_   9. _yarn_
2. _tar_   10. _far_
3. _dark_   11. _spark_
4. _bar_   12. _car_
5. _shark_   13. _star_
6. _jar_   14. _bark_
7. _scar_   15. _Mark_
8. _mark_   16. _park_

6. Read the sentences.
Review words: barn, large, market

1. Get a jar of jelly at the market.
2. The park is not far from the school.
3. Fern gets good marks in her math class.
4. When it is dark, we look at the stars.
5. The pup is barking. He is not far off.
6. I am making a hat out of dark red yarn.
7. Ted put a bar under the box to lift it.
8. Sparks fell from the burning barn.
9. Sharks are very large fish.
10. Kim parked her car next to the barn.
11. The street is covered with black tar.
12. Mark had lunch at the snack bar.
13. He has a large scar on his leg.
14. A lark is singing in the park.
15. That tree has a thick bark.
16. We cannot go very far in this car.

119

Practice 47-B: ar

1. **ar**

arm

farm

large

2. Write the letters you hear.

	ar		**ra**	
1. c	_ar_ d	5. sc	_ar_ f	
2. b	_ra_ n	6. b	_ra_ g	
3.	_ra_ sh	7. f	_ar_ m	
4.	_ar_ m	8. g	_ra_ ss	

3. Write the letters and say the word.

ar	**ar**
c _ar_ d	h _ar_ m
gu _ar_ d	ch _ar_ m
h _ar_ d	b _ar_ ge
l _ar_ d	l _ar_ ge
y _ar_ d	M _ar_ ge
sc _ar_ f	ch _ar_ ge
C _ar_ l	h _ar_ p
sn _ar_ l	sh _ar_ p

4. Read the words.

sharp	hard
harp	yard
large	guard
charge	lard
barge	card
Marge	charm
snarl	harm
Carl	scarf

5. Write the word you hear.

1.	_yard_	9.	_scarf_
2.	_harp_	10.	_charge_
3.	_barge_	11.	_Carl_
4.	_card_	12.	_sharp_
5.	_Marge_	13.	_guard_
6.	_harm_	14.	_large_
7.	_snarl_	15.	_hard_
8.	_lard_	16.	_charm_

6. Read the sentences.
Review words: arm, farm, farmer, garden

1. Marge is sending Carl a birthday card.
2. We have a large barnyard on our farm.
3. The pup snarls at me. Will it harm me?
4. My wife plants a garden in the yard.
5. Large barges carry goods up the river.
6. Marge has her good luck charm with her.
7. The farmer works hard on his farm.
8. The bark on that tree is hard.
9. It has a sharp edge. It cuts well.
10. Carl hands the clerk his charge card.
11. Lard is the fat that comes from pigs.
12. A large yarn scarf covers her head.
13. Marge can play the harp.
14. Our garden is six yards by ten yards.
15. Armed guards kept him from harm.
16. There is no charge for parking there.

120

Note: The word *march* is used both as a common and proper noun.

Practice 47-C: ar

1. **ar**

   start

   Arthur

   march

2. Write the letters you hear.

	ar	ra			
1. t	_ra_ p		5. st	_ar_ ch	
2. d	_ar_ t		6. b	_ra_ t	
3. c	_ra_ b		7. t	_ra_ sh	
4. b	_ar_ k		8. p	_ar_ t	

3. Write the letters and say the word.

ar		ar	
_ar_ t		c _ar_ ve	
c _ar_ t		st _ar_ ve	
d _ar_ t		h _ar_ sh	
p _ar_ t		m _ar_ sh	
t _ar_ t		_ar_ ch	
ch _ar_ t		m _ar_ ch	
sm _ar_ t		M _ar_ ch	
st _ar_ t		st _ar_ ch	

4. Read the words.

part	marsh
chart	harsh
art	March
start	arch
cart	starch
smart	march
dart	carve
tart	starve

5. Write the word you hear.

1. march	9. starch
2. dart	10. cart
3. chart	11. harsh
4. carve	12. tart
5. start	13. starve
6. arch	14. part
7. marsh	15. March
8. art	16. smart

6. Read the sentences.
   New words: love, army, Barb
   Review words: Arthur, Indian

   1. Put a jar of nuts in the shopping cart.
   2. The army started marching up the hill.
   3. Mom puts starch in Dad's shirts.
   4. Arthur loves his arts and crafts class.
   5. Barb is making little apple tarts.
   6. Water covers a large part of the marsh.
   7. Dad started to carve the hen.
   8. In March, the army ended the draft.
   9. My sister Barb loves to play darts.
   10. Arthur is smart. He makes good marks.
   11. What part do you act in the play?
   12. Her red, chapped hands felt harsh.
   13. The head of the army is studying charts.
   14. My cat arched her back and hissed.
   15. I am starved! When do we have lunch?
   16. Barb loves to study Indian art.

121

156

The Sound *or* in Practices 48-A and 48-B

The *or* practices follow exactly the same procedure as the previous *vowel-r* practices. There is just one thing to keep in mind about the *or* sound /or/, however. The sound is actually a *long* vowel sound, or close to it. The /or/ sound is included here so that S. can contrast it with the other *r*-controlled vowels, and practice blending the sound with consonant sounds that come before it and after it. You may want to call S.'s attention to this different sound. Make sure S. can recognize the /or/ sound and pronounce it correctly.

Although practices 48-A and 48-B have many *or* words, those practices do not include words which are spelled with *ore* or *oar*. *Ore* and *oar* words will be covered in the next workbook in this series, *Focus on Phonics-3*. They are saved for that workbook because they illustrate the long vowel rules well. You might want to explain to S. why he will study these words later if he asks about them. Or if S. has already studied long vowels, and you want to present these words to him, there is a brief list below for your reference. Also included in the list are words having the /or/ sound spelled with *oor* and *our:*

/or/ spelled *ore:* bore, core, more, pore, sore, tore, wore, shore, chore, score, snore, spore, store, swore.

/or/ spelled *oar:* oar, soar, roar, board, hoard.

/or/ spelled *oor:* door, poor, floor.

/or/ spelled *our:* four, pour, mourn, court, course.

Practice 48-A: or

1. **or**

    or

    for

    corn

2. Write the letters you hear.

        or   **ro**

1. b _or_ n   5. c _or_ d
2. t _ro_ t   6. b _ro_ th
3. f _or_ k   7. _ro_ b
4. p _ro_ p   8. t _or_ n

3. Write the letters and say the word.

    or   **or**

  _or_   b _or_ n
c _or_ d   c _or_ n
F _or_ d   h _or_ n
l _or_ d   t _or_ n
c _or_ k   w _or_ n
f _or_ k   th _or_ n
p _or_ k   sc _or_ n
st _or_ k   sw _or_ n

4. Read the words.

torn	or
corn	fork
sworn	stork
thorn	cork
horn	pork
scorn	Ford
worn	cord
born	lord

5. Write the word you hear.

1.	_fork_	9.	_corn_
2.	_worn_	10.	_thorn_
3.	_cord_	11.	_pork_
4.	_born_	12.	_lord_
5.	_scorn_	13.	_horn_
6.	_or_	14.	_cork_
7.	_Ford_	15.	_sworn_
8.	_stork_	16.	_torn_

6. Read the sentences.
New words: morning, new
Review word: York

1. My new Ford has a good horn!
2. The plant is covered with sharp thorns.
3. We were born in New York City.
4. Give me a fork. I will carve this pork.
5. She was sworn into office this morning.
6. Ed trips over the cord of the TV set.
7. Jack has no job, but do not scorn him.
8. He has not worn that shirt. It is torn.
9. Serve corn or bread with the pork.
10. The stork visited them this morning!
    A new baby was born to them!
11. Barb asks, "Lord God, help us!"
12. Put the dishes and forks in the sink.
13. The farmer picks corn every morning.
14. Mark plays his new horn in the band.
15. Put the cork back in to stop it up.

122

Practice 48-B: or

1. **or**

or

for

short

2. Write the letters you hear.

or   ro

1. c __ro__ p
2. f __or__ m
3. p __or__ t
4. __ro__ t

5. t __or__ ch
6. d __ro__ p
7. f __or__ t
8. p __ro__ m

3. Write the letters and say the word.

or

f __or__ t
p __or__ t
s __or__ t
sh __or__ t
sp __or__ t
sn __or__ t
f __or__ m
st __or__ m

or

f __or__ ce
h __or__ se
p __or__ ch
t __or__ ch
sc __or__ ch
f __or__ th
n __or__ th
f __or__ ge

4. Read the words.

torch	forge
porch	force
scorch	sort
storm	port
form	short
horse	snort
north	fort
forth	sport

5. Write the word you hear.

1. __short__
2. __north__
3. __force__
4. __storm__
5. __torch__
6. __port__
7. __forge__
8. __snort__
9. __fort__
10. __horse__
11. __sport__
12. __scorch__
13. __forth__
14. __sort__
15. __porch__
16. __form__

6. Read the sentences.

1. Marge is sitting out on the porch.
2. I fill out the short form to pay taxes.
   I have to force myself to do it.
3. The army marched north to the fort.
4. What sort of sports do you like best?
5. The horse lifted his head and snorted.
6. Carl forged my name on a check.
7. When it got dark, Ed lit a torch.
8. There is a bad storm north of us.
9. I scorched the shirt. It is burned.
10. Bill is the best cop on the force.
11. I am short, but I play many sports.
12. The ship is coming into port.
13. We are forming a sports club.
14. The women are sorting the letters.
15. The horse went forth into the storm.

123

Practice 49: Review of Vowels + *r*

T. says: In this practice, you will review the *r* combinations you have studied: *e-r, i-r, u-r, a-r,* and *o-r.*

1 Look at the picture and say the word. Then write the letters for the sounds you hear.

T. says: Look at the picture and say the word.

Then fill in the letters that make the sound you hear.

Be sure S. pronounces each word correctly. S. fills in the *r* combination that makes the sounds he hears. Since *er, ir,* and *ur* all sound alike, S. must remember from studying those three practices which combination goes with which word.

2 Circle all the words that are the same as the first one.

T. says: Circle all the words that are the same as the first. Work from left to right.

This is primarily a *visual* discrimination exercise. It is useful for giving evidence of visual problems like poor vision, directional problems, and reversals of letters and words. It is very important for you to note the kinds of errors S. makes. Some of the incorrect words are new to S., but they *look* like the word to be circled. In some cases, an incorrect word is the same as the circled word except for the vowel. If S. makes an error by circling these words, he is probably not noticing the vowels or the *r* combinations in words. If S. makes many mistakes in this visual discrimination exercise (three or more), you should check further for visual problems.

3 Fill in the blanks with *-er, -ir, -ur, -ar,* or *-or* to make a word.

T. says: The words listed below have some letters missing.

You have had these words before.

You must fill in *e-r, i-r, u-r, a-r,* or *o-r* in each one to make a word.

Then read the word.

For some words, S. may have to try the *r* combinations one by one to see which one fits (only one is possible). S. should recognize a word after he fills in the right combination, since he has studied the words before. He must use his memory as well as his knowledge of sounds, since *er, ir,* and *ur* all sound alike.

4 Use these words to fill in the blanks.

T. says: Here are eight words that you have seen before. (Point to words.)

They have the *r* combinations that you are reviewing.

Read the words. (Go over the words and their meanings with S.)

Now you will use those eight words in sentences.

Read each sentence and fill in the word that makes sense.

Use each word just once.

160

Practice 49: Review of Vowels + r: er, ir, ur, ar, or

1. Look at the picture and say the word. Then write the letters for the sounds you hear.

1.

sk _ir_ t

3.

f _er_ n

5.

p _ur_ se

2.

st _ar_

4.

c _or_ n

6.

y _ar_ n

2. Circle all the words that are the same as the first one.

form	(form)	from	(form)	farm	(form)	force
chart	cart	charm	starch	(chart)	arch	start
herd	heard	hard	(herd)	her	(herd)	hers
sort	snort	(sort)	store	short	storm	(sort)
turn	(turn)	torn	runt	burn	(turn)	term
part	pert	park	(part)	tarp	port	(part)

3. Fill in the blanks with *er, ir, ur, ar,* or *or* to make a word.

1. ch _ar_ m
2. _ur_ ge
3. sn _or_ t
4. j _er_ k
5. b _ur_ p
6. c _or_ n
7. y _ar_ d
8. tw _ir_ l
9. t _er_ m

4. Use these words to fill in the blanks:

birth   pork   barn   term
torn   church   sharp   charge

1. Carl gives the clerk his **charge** card to pay for the scarf.
2. Barb has not worn the skirt since it got **torn** .
3. For dinner, Mark had **pork** , corn, and tarts.
4. The farmer led his horse into a large **barn** .
5. A nurse helped Marge with her first baby's **birth** .
6. The Ford swerved on the **sharp** curve.
7. Arthur has started to serve his third **term** in office.
8. Fern parked her car not far from the **church** .

124

Practice 50: *ear* and *wor*

This practice introduces some words that have the sound /er/ spelled *e-a-r* and the sound /wer/ spelled *w-o-r*.

T. says: By now you've learned many words that have the /er/ sound.

Those words were spelled with *e-r, i-r, or u-r.*

In this practice, you will learn some other words that have the /er/ sound.

1

T. says: The words in the first group are spelled with *e-a-r* plus another consonant. (Point to *heard* at the top of the page.)

But you will read them as if they had no *a,* as if they were spelled with *e-r,* instead of *e-a-r.*

They have the *e-r* sound /er/ in them.

You have seen this word before. (Point to *heard* again.)

What is it? [S: heard] Good.

In *heard,* the *e-a-r* sounds like /er/.

What do you think this word is? (Point to the second word.)

[S: learn] Good. (Help S. sound out the word if he needs help.)

Can you see that the *e-a-r* makes the /er/ sound in *learn*?

2 Circle the word you hear.

T. says: In the words you've studied with *o-r,* the *o-r* makes the sound /or/.

But that's not true for most words spelled *w-o-r.* (Point to *wor.*)

In these words, the *w-o-r* sounds like this: /wer/.

Say the sound /wer/. [/wer/] Right.

The two words listed below *wor* are words you've seen before.

What is this word? (Point to *word.*) [S: word] Good.

What is this word? (Point to *work.*) [S: work] Right.

Can you hear that in both *word* and *work,* the *w-o-r* sounds like /wer/?

Now let's look at some more *e-a-r* and *w-o-r* words.

3 Write the letters and say the word.

T. says: What does *e-a-r* sound like when it is followed by another consonant?

[S: /er/] Good.

You can make new words that have the /er/ sound in them.

They are spelled with *e-a-r.* (Point to *ear* at the top of the first column.)

If I have *h* and then *e-a-r* (write these letters in), and then *d,*

I have the sounds /h/, /er/, /d/.

Say those sounds as I point to the letters.

(Point to *h.*) [S: /h/] (Point to *e-a-r.*) [S: /er/] (Point to *d.*) [S: /d/]

Now blend those sounds together into a word. [S: heard] Good.

(Help S. if he has trouble.)

T. says: The next word is a name. *E-a-r* sounds like /er/. (Point to the letters that are written in.)

And *l* sounds like/l/. (Point to *l.*)

Say those sounds as I point to them.

(Point to *Ear.*) [S: /er/] (Point to *l.*) [S: /l/]

Can you blend those sounds together into a word?

[S: Earl] Good. (Help S. if he has trouble.)

Now let's go through the rest of the words in this column.

All the words have the sound /er/ spelled with *e-a-r.*

You write the letters and read the words.

When S. has finished the first column, proceed to the second.

T. says: What does *w-o-r* sound like when it is followed by another consonant?

[S: /wer/] Good.

You can make new words that have the /wer/ sound in them.

They all start with *w-o-r.*

If I write *w-o-r* before *d* (write these letters in), I have the sounds /wer/ and /d/.

Say those sounds as I point to the letters.

(Point to *w-o-r.*) [S: /wer/] (Point to *d.*) [S: /d/] Good.

Now blend those sounds together into a word. [S: word] Good.

(Help S. if he has trouble.)

Now let's go through the rest of the words.

All the words have the sound /wer/ spelled with *w-o-r.*

You write the letters and read the words.

Help S. with the rest of the words. Two of them, *worst* and *world,* have consonant blends after *wor.*

4 5 6

For the rest of the practice, follow the same procedure as for the other *vowel-r* practices or the blend practices.

162

Practice 50: ear and wor

1. **ear = /er/** **wor = /wer/**

    heard   word

    learn   work

2. Circle the word you hear.

   1. word   (cord)
   2. (heard)   hard
   3. (work)   fork
   4. yearn   (yarn)
   5. earth   (art)
   6. (worm)   form
   7. (worst)   was
   8. worth   (north)

3. Write the letters and say the word.

ear	wor
h _ear_ d	_wor_ d
Ear l	_wor_ k
p _ear_ l	_wor_ m
ear n	_wor_ se
l _ear_ n	_wor_ st
y _ear_ n	_wor_ th
s _ear_ ch	_wor_ ld
ear th	

4. Read the words.

learn	worm
earn	worth
yearn	worse
pearl	worst
Earl	word
earth	world
search	work
heard	

5. Write the word you hear.

   1. _pearl_   9. _search_
   2. _work_   10. _world_
   3. _learn_   11. _heard_
   4. _worth_   12. _worst_
   5. _Earl_   13. _earth_
   6. _worse_   14. _word_
   7. _yearn_   15. _earn_
   8. _worm_

6. Read the sentences.
   New words: worry, about

   1. Earl works to earn money.
   2. That string of pearls is worth a lot.
   3. I yearn to visit the rest of the world.
   4. Earl is learning to spell many words.
   5. Ned is searching for worms for fishing.
   6. Worrying about it just makes it worse.
   7. The cops search for the missing pearls.
   8. This car is the worst! It never works!
   9. I have not heard a word he said.
   10. Do not worry! The worst is over!
   11. The worms are digging in the earth.
   12. She earns about fifty dollars a day.
   13. We heard about Earl. He is very sick.
       We worry that he will get worse.
   14. We learned about the earth's crust.
   15. This work is not worth doing.

125

Practice 51: Compound words

Note: S. has already been introduced to compound words and two-syllable words in Practices 14-A and 14-B of Part A of this workbook, so this may be a review for him. If he knows them well, you may want to skip this introductory section and go right to part 1. The words used in Practices 51 and 52 have consonant blends.

Before discussing compound words, introduce S. to the idea of syllables.

T. says: You will soon find yourself reading bigger words.

The bigger words have two or more parts.

We call the parts *syllables*.

The syllables are the beats or parts you hear when you say the word.

Let me give you some examples.

These words have only one beat when you say them, even though there are many sounds in the word: (Clap once as you say each word.) *blast drill spin gift pump truck land stop*

Each of these words has *one* syllable.

These words have two beats when you say them: (Clap twice with each word.)

basket kitchen building garden color plenty

Each of these words has *two* syllables.

A word has a syllable *for every vowel sound you hear.* But if it's hard for you to tell the number of vowel sounds in the word, say the word and listen to the number of beats or parts in it.

When S. understands what syllables are, see whether he can identify the number of syllables in the words he hears.

T. says: Now I will read you some words you've had in your reading.

You listen and tell me how many syllables each word has.

You can say the word after me or clap if you want to.

mask (1)	went (1)
baby (2)	Indian (3)
grandmother (3)	list (1)
stitch (1)	never (1)
ready (2)	twenty (2)
blink (1)	family (3)
market (2)	grip (1)
spell (1)	farmer (2)

If S. makes a mistake, repeat the word slowly and clap as you say it. When S. understands syllables well, go on to compound words.

1 Look at these compound words.

T. says: Now you'll figure out some big words that have two or more syllables.

They are called *compound words*.

Compound words are big words made out of two smaller words.

Look at the compound words at the top of this page. (Point to words.)

Can you see the two smaller words in each of the big words?

The smaller words are written next to the compound words.

In a compound word, the two little words are right together with no space in between them.

Go over the examples of compound words.

2 Put the two words together to make a compound word. Read the word.

T. says: Now look at these words.

Put the two smaller words together to make a compound word.

Write them in the blanks.

Read the smaller words and the compound word.

Check S.'s work as he reads the words. You may want to discuss the meanings of the words.

3 Find the two smaller words in each compound word. Write them in the blanks. Read the smaller words and the compound word.

T. says: Now look at these compound words.

Find the two smaller words in each compound word.

Write them in the blanks.

Read the smaller words and the compound word.

4 Make compound words. Match each word on the left with a word on the right. Write the compound word in the blank.

T. says: These are words you've read before.

Make a compound word with each of these words (point to the words on the left) by finding another word over here to go with it (point to the words on the right).

Write the compound word in the blank, next to the first word. The first one is done for you.

Then read the compound words you've made.

S. may want to read through the lists of words in each group before starting. Check S.'s work as you have him read the words. You may want to discuss the meanings of the compound words.

After S. finishes all of the exercises, you may have him read through all the compound words and write the number of syllables in each word.

Practice 51: Compound Words

1. Look at these compound words.

sunlamp   sun   lamp   hairbrush   hair   brush

fingerprint   finger   print   inchworm   inch   worm

slingshot   sling   shot   quicksand   quick   sand

2. Put the two words together to make a compound word. Read the word.

hand stand _handstand_   land mark _landmark_   sand paper _sandpaper_

work bench _workbench_   egg plant _eggplant_   out smart _outsmart_

left over _leftover_   her self _herself_   sun glasses _sunglasses_

sports cast _sportscast_   back track _backtrack_   wind storm _windstorm_

3. Find the two smaller words in each compound word. Write them in the blanks. Read the smaller words and the compound word.

riverbank _river_ _bank_   cornstarch _corn_ _starch_

stopwatch _stop_ _watch_   underwater _under_ _water_

snapshot _snap_ _shot_   pitchfork _pitch_ _fork_

drumstick _drum_ _stick_   standstill _stand_ _still_

windchill _wind_ _chill_   yardstick _yard_ _stick_

grandfather _grand_ _father_   blacksmith _black_ _smith_

4. Make compound words. Match each word on the left with a word on the right. Write the compound word in the blank. The first one is done for you.

flash _flashback_ stop   silk _silkworm_ mother

witch _witchcraft_ mark   step _stepmother_ worm

short _shortstop_ car   play _plaything_ born

birth _birthmark_ back   milk _milkman_ west

street _streetcar_ grass   first _firstborn_ man

crab _crabgrass_ craft   north _northwest_ thing

126

Practice 52: Two-syllable Words

Note: Put the stress on the **boldface** syllables when you pronounce the words.

1

T. says: You have learned to sound out many words with short vowels and blends.

This practice will help you sound out many big words, too.

Look at the big words below. (Point to the words.)

The syllable that is in *boldface type* is the *stressed* one.

The *stressed* syllable is the one that has the emphasis, or the hardest beat when you say the word.

The syllable that is not in *boldface type* is the *unstressed* one.

It has less emphasis when you say it.

Using what you have learned about sounding out words, sound out the syllables and figure out each word.

Look at this word. (Point to *plastic*.)

There's a *c* at the end of the word.

At the end of a word, *c* makes the sound /k/.

How would you say the first syllable? [S: /plas/] Good.

And the second syllable? [S: /tic/] Good.

Now put them together. What's the word? [S: plastic] Good.

(Help S. sound out the syllables if necessary.)

(The word *plastic* is used as an example because S. is used to seeing the ending sound /k/ spelled with a *ck* in many one-syllable words. S. should know that the sound /k/ at the end of many two-syllable words is spelled with just a *c*.)

You can see that the first syllable is *stressed*.

It has the hardest beat. It gets the emphasis.

Can you hear how the first syllable is emphasized when you say the word *plastic*? You don't say /plas **tic**/. You say /**plas** tic/.

Can you hear the difference?

Now look at this word. (Point to *skillet*.)

How would you say the first syllable? [S: /skil/] Good.

This syllable is the *stressed* one.

The next syllable is unstressed.

In many unstressed syllables, the vowel is pronounced like a short *u:* /u/.

In this word, the vowel is pronounced like a short *u:* /uh/.

How would you say this syllable? (Point to *let*.) [S: /lut/] Good.

So how do you say the word? [S: skillet] Good.

T. says: Notice that there are two *l's* in the middle of the word.

When you put the two syllables together and say the word, you say just one /l/ sound.

How do you say this word again? (Point to *skillet*.) [S: skillet] Good.

(The term for the unstressed vowel sound is *schwa*. It is shown in dictionaries as an upside down *e*. You may want to show S. some examples from dictionaries.)

Continue with part 1, helping S. where necessary.

2 Read the word first. Then read the sentence.

T. says: Now you will read several other big words.

These words have been divided into syllables.

Sound out the syllables and figure out each word.

Remember that the boldface syllable is the *stressed* one.

Then read the sentence that uses that word.

3 Read the word. Fill in the blank. Read the sentence.

T. says: Here are some more new words.

Read each word and write it in the blank.

Then read the sentence with that word.

4 Read the story.

T. says: Here is a story with many of the new words you've learned in it.

Read the story.

5 Fill in each blank with one of these words.

T. says: On the left are six more new words.

Figure out those words.

Then use each of those words just once in one of the sentences at the right.

Practice 52: Two-Syllable Words

1. The big words below have been divided into syllables. Using what you have learned about sounding out words, sound out the syllables, and figure out each word.

plastic　　/**plas** tic/　　skillet　/**skil** lut/　　clever　/**clev** er/　　intend　/in **tend**/

2. Read the word first. Then read the sentence.

1. constant	/**con** stant/	We cannot stand that <u>constant</u> yelling!
2. product	/**prod** uct/	This shop sells a good <u>product</u> for less.
3. clinic	/**clin** ic/	This nurse works in a big <u>clinic</u>.
4. credit	/**cred** it/	Dad hands the clerk his <u>credit</u> card.
5. intend	/in **tend**/	Jan does not <u>intend</u> to marry Frank.
6. skillet	/**skil** lut/	Melt the butter in the hot <u>skillet</u>.
7. profit	/**prof** ut/	Dan made a <u>profit</u> on the stock market.

3. Read the word. Fill in the blank. Read the sentence.

1. pumpkin	/**pump** kin/	Mom is making _____ *pumpkin* _____ bread.
2. current	/**cur** runt/	Yesterday's newspaper is not _____ *current* _____.
3. selfish	/**self** ish/	Do not be _____ *selfish* _____! Give it to me!
4. problem	/**prob** lum/	I tell my _____ *problem* _____ to my best friend.
5. suburb	/**sub** urb/	They live in a _____ *suburb* _____ of a big city.
6. plastic	/**plas** tic/	The cups and dishes are _____ *plastic* _____.

4. Read the story.

My Aunt Marge runs a factory in the suburbs.
Her factory makes pots, pans, and skillets.
She is working on her current product, a new skillet.
She says, "Ours will be the best product on the market!
We will run constant tests on it to get rid of any problems."
I have to give Aunt Marge a lot of credit.
She is smart and a hard worker.
She does not just make skillets.
She thinks up clever ads to sell them.
As you can guess, my aunt's factory makes a big profit!

5. Fill in each blank with one of these words.

frantic	/**fran** tic/	1. A cop is stopping the _____ *traffic* _____.
sandwich	/**sand** wich/	2. The _____ *squirrel* _____ hid some nuts.
trumpet	/**trum** put/	3. Mother was _____ *frantic* _____ with worry.
traffic	/**traf** fic/	4. Fran plays a _____ *trumpet* _____ in the band.
squirrel	/**squir** rul/	5. Put the _____ *sandwich* _____ in a plastic bag.
gravel	/**grav** ul/	6. The dump truck is carrying _____ *gravel* _____.

127

Practice 53-A: CC-*le* Words with a Double Consonant in the Middle

T. says: You have had practice sounding out some compound words and other two-syllable words. In the next two practices, you will learn to read some more two-syllable words.

All these words will have something in common.

They will have two consonants and an *l-e* at the end of the word.

In this practice, the two consonants will have the same sound.

1

T. says: Look at the words in this part.

They have been divided into syllables. Let's sound them out.

You have seen this word. What is it? (Point to *apple*.)

[S: apple] Good.

Apple is divided into syllables here. (Point to syllables.)

The first syllable, /ap/, is the *stressed* syllable.

Remember, the *stressed* syllable is the one that gets the emphasis when you say the word. It has the hardest beat.

Now, at the end of a word, *l-e* makes the sound /ul/.

Say /ul/. [S: /ul/] Good.

Now, what is the first syllable? (Point to **ap**.)
[S: /ap/]

What is the second syllable? (Point to *pul*.)
[S: /pul/]

Notice that *apple* has two *p*'s in the middle.

When you put the two syllables together and say the word, you say just one /p/ sound.

How do you say this word again? (Point to *apple*.)
[S: apple] Good.

All the words you will learn in these two practices end with *l-e*.

Remember that at the end of a word, *l-e* makes the sound /ul/.

The syllable before /ul/ is always *stressed*.

Go over the familiar word *little* and the new word *shuffle* the same way. Then explain the word *tickle* this way:

T. says: All of the words in this practice have a double consonant before the *l-e,* except for the words that end *c-k-l-e.*

The letters *c-k* together are like a double consonant.

They make the same sound, /k/.

(Point to **tic**.) How do you say this syllable?
[S: /tic/] Good.

You have *k-l-e* at the end of the word. Point to **kle**. What does that sound like?

[S: /kul/] Good.

There is a /k/ sound in each syllable, but when you put the two syllables together and say the word, you say just one /k/ sound.

So how do you say the word? [S: tickle] Right.

2 Read the word first. Then read the sentence.

T. says: Now you will read some other words like those you just learned.

They have been divided into syllables.

Sound out the syllables and figure out each word.

Remember that *l-e* at the end of a word makes the sound /ul/.

Remember that the syllable *before* the *l-e* is the stressed one.

Then read the sentence that uses that word.

3 Read the word. Fill in the blank. Read the sentence.

T. says: Here are some more new words.

Read each word and write it in the blank.

Then read the sentence with that word.

4 Read the story.

T. says: Here is a story with many of the new words you've learned in it.

Read the story.

5 Fill in each blank with one of the -*le* words.

T. says: On the left are six more new words.

Figure out those words.

Then use each word just once in one of the sentences at the right.

Then read the sentences.

168

Practice 53-A: CC-le Words with a Double Consonant in the Middle

1. The big words below have been divided into syllables. Using what you have learned about sounding out words, sound out the syllables and figure out the words.

      apple   /**ap** pul/   little /**lit** tul/   shuffle /**shuf** ful/   tickle /**tic** kul/

2. Read the word first. Then read the sentence.

1. saddle	/**sad** dul/	<u>Saddle</u> up the horses.
2. wiggle	/**wig** gul/	The baby <u>wiggles</u> his legs.
3. pickle	/**pic** kul/	Put some <u>pickles</u> on the bun.
4. kettle	/**ket** tul/	Mom is making jelly in a big <u>kettle</u>.
5. puddle	/**pud** dul/	John fell in the <u>puddle</u> and got wet.
6. tackle	/**tac** kul/	Ed takes his <u>tackle</u> box when he fishes.
7. nibble	/**nib** bul/	My son <u>nibbles</u> on the chips.

3. Read the word. Fill in the blank. Read the sentence.

1. bottle	/**bot** tul/	A _____bottle_____ of ink is on his desk.
2. tickle	/**tic** kul/	My baby laughs when I _____tickle_____ her.
3. rattle	/**rat** tul/	The baby plays with a _____rattle_____ .
4. puzzle	/**puz** zul/	Did you put the _____puzzle_____ together?
5. struggle	/**strug** gul/	Dan had to _____struggle_____ to pass the test.
6. settle	/**set** tul/	Fred wants to _____settle_____ in this city.

4. Read the story.

My little son Mark is three.
Yesterday I was tickling him.
He wiggled out of my arms and ran out into the yard.
Then he sat down in a mud puddle!
After lunch, I said, "Settle down with a puzzle."
"No!" Mark said. He did not want any puzzles.
I heard a rattle. Mark was playing with my pans and kettles.
I said "Stop!" and handed him an apple to nibble on.
Next I heard a crash! He had dropped a bottle of pickles.
Living with a boy of three can be a struggle!
But I want another kid just like him!

5. Fill in each blank with one of these -le words.

buckle	/**buc** kul/	1. Give me a pack of _____bubble_____ gum.
cattle	/**cat** tul/	2. I rest in the _____middle_____ of the day.
raffle	/**raf** ful/	3. The river has lots of _____ripple_____s.
bubble	/**bub** bul/	4. Did Stan win a car in the _____raffle_____?
middle	/**mid** dul/	5. The belt _____buckle_____ is made of brass.
ripple	/**rip** pul/	6. Ted has a large herd of _____cattle_____.

128

Practice 53-B: CC-*le* Words with Two Different Consonants in the Middle

T. says: In this practice, like the last one, you will sound out more words that end with two consonants and an *l-e.*

But in this practice, there are two different consonants before the *l-e.*

In all of these words, the syllable before the *l-e* is the stressed syllable.

1

T. says: Let's look at the words in this part.

They have been divided into syllables. Let's sound them out.

Here is the first word. (Point to *handle.*)

How would you say the first syllable, *h-a-n?* [S: /han/] Good.

Now here's *d-l-e.*

Remember that *l-e* at the end of a word makes the sound /ul/.

How do you say *d-l-e?* [S: /dul/] Good.

Can you put the syllables together to make a word?

[S: handle] Good.

Help S. if he has trouble. Repeat the process with the next word, *gamble.*

T. says: The next word has an *n-g* in it. (Point to *single.*)

When a word ends with *n-g-l-e,* the *g* has two jobs.

First, it is part of *n-g,* which makes the sound /ng/. So the first syllable of this word is /sing/.

Then *g* has the sound /g/ in the *g-l-e* syllable. So, the second syllable is /gul/.

How do you say this syllable? (Point to **sing.**) [S: /sing/]

How do you say this syllable? (Point to /gul/.) [S: /gul/]

Can you put the syllables together to make a word? [S: single] Good.

The next word ends with *n-k-l-e.* (Point to *ankle.*)

Before *k, n* makes the sound /ng/.

So this syllable (point to **ang**) is pronounced /ang/.

T. says: Say /ang/. [S: /ang/] Good.

The next syllable is *k-l-e.*

How do you say that? [S: /kul/] Good.

Can you put the two syllables together to make a word?

[S: ankle] Right.

Now look at the last word. (Point to *whistle.*)

It ends with *s-t-l-e.* The *t* is silent.

In all words that end *s-t-l-e,* the *t* is silent.

How do you say this syllable? (Point to **whis.**) [S: /whis/] Good.

How do you say this syllable? (Point to *le.*) [S: /ul/] Right.

Can you put the syllables together to make a word?

Remember, the *t* is silent.

[S: whistle] Good.

2 Read the word first. Then read the sentence.

T. says: Now you will read some more words like those you just learned.

They have been divided into syllables.

Sound out the syllables and figure out each word.

Remember that the syllable before the *l-e* is the stressed one.

Then read the sentence that uses that word.

3 Read the word. Fill in the blank. Read the sentence.

T. says: Here are some new words.

Read each word and write it in the blank.

Then read the sentence that uses that word.

4 Fill in each blank with one of the -*le* words.

T. says: On the left are seven more words.

Figure out those words.

Then use each word just once in one of the sentences at the right.

5 *r-c-le* words. Read the word and the sentence.

T. says: These words have an *r* before the consonant *l*-e.

Remember that *a-r* sounds like /ar/.

Remember that *e-r, i-r,* and *u-r* all sound like /er/.

After you figure out each word, read the sentence that uses that word.

170

Practice 53-B: CC-le Words with Two Different Consonants in the Middle

1. The big words below have been divided into syllables. Sound out the syllables and figure out the words.

handle /**han** dul/   gamble /**gam** bul/   single /**sing** gul/   ankle /**ang** kul/   whistle /**whis** ul/

2. Read the word first. Then read the sentence.

   1. tangle   /**tang** gul/   The yarn is <u>tangled</u> up.
   2. stumble   /**stum** bul/   Dad <u>stumbled</u> over the trash can.
   3. sample   /**sam** pul/   I will <u>sample</u> the punch.
   4. twinkle   /**twing** kul/   We look at the stars <u>twinkle.</u>
   5. swindle   /**swin** dul/   He <u>swindled</u> her out of her money.
   6. candle   /**can** dul/   It was dark, so I lit a <u>candle.</u>
   7. gamble   /**gam** bul/   Mark never wins when he <u>gambles.</u>

3. Read the word. Fill in the blank. Read the sentence.

   1. simple   /**sim** pul/   This math is _____simple_____, not hard.
   2. jungle   /**jung** gul/   The men walked out of the _____jungle_____ .
   3. scramble   /**scram** bul/   _____Scramble_____ the eggs for dinner.
   4. bundle   /**bun** dul/   Kim carries a _____bundle_____ under her arm.
   5. angle   /**ang** gul/   Cut it on an _____angle_____ .
   6. tremble   /**trem** bul/   Her hands started to _____tremble_____ .

4. Fill in each blank with one of the *-le* words.

handle	/**han** dul/	1. The king lives in a _____castle_____ .
thimble	/**thim** bul/	2. They go to church in the _____temple_____ .
ankle	/**ang** kul/	3. Pick it up by the _____handle_____ .
castle	/**cas** ul/	4. Hank is not married. He is _____single_____ .
temple	/**tem** pul/	5. Chuck fell and turned his _____ankle_____ .
single	/**sing** gul/	6. The _____thimble_____ is big for my finger.
uncle	/**ung** kul/	7. _____Uncle_____ Bob is Dad's brother.

5. *r-C-le* words. Read the word and the sentence.

   1. turtle   /**tur** tul/   Barb gets a <u>turtle</u> at the pet shop.
   2. marble   /**mar** bul/   The children are playing <u>marbles.</u>
   3. girdle   /**gir** dul/   They sell <u>girdles</u> at the dress shop.
   4. sparkle   /**spar** kul/   Your ring <u>sparkles</u>!
   5. purple   /**pur** pul/   Her skirt is pink and <u>purple.</u>
   6. startle   /**star** tul/   The telephone ring <u>startled</u> me.

129

Shopping at the Department Store

New words: Carter, apartment, department, store, handle

Marge Carter lives in a large apartment.
She says, "This is the day to go shopping.
I will go to the new department store I have heard about.
A person can get many things in a large department store."

Marge hurries out of the apartment.
She starts her car and heads for the department store.
The department store is on North First Street.
It is not far from the apartment.
She turns her car into the large parking lot and parks.

Marge gets a cart and starts shopping.
First Marge looks at a box of gift cards. It is marked $2.00.
She puts the cards in her cart.
Then she picks up some brushes.
"My son Carl will want some brushes for his art class," she says.

The third thing she picks up is a scarf.
The scarf is made of red yarn.
"My girl Barb will like this scarf," she says.

Then Marge looks at some shirts.
She thinks, "Mark wants a new sports shirt. His red one is torn."
She puts a shirt in the cart.

Next she picks out some kitchen curtains.
And she picks up some jars for canning.
Last she picks up some ferns and other plants for the apartment.

The clerk asks Marge, "Will this be cash or charge?"

Marge says, "I am short of cash."

She takes a charge card out of her purse and hands it to the clerk.
"It is smart of me to pay with my charge card."

"Yes," says the woman in back of her. "It can be smart to charge it.
But some cannot handle charge cards very well.
They charge many large bills.
They can pay for just part of their bills.
But they charge and charge until it gets hard for them to pay.
When they cannot pay, the store takes back their things.
Their charge cards have hurt them."

"Yes," Marge says. "You have to watch out when you charge things.
I am glad I can pay for what I charge.
Charge cards will never harm me.
I can handle them well."

Marge hurries out of the store with two large bags in her arms.
She thinks, "You have to be pretty smart just to shop in a department store!"

130

APPENDIXES:

Appendix A: Phonics, Phonemic Awareness, and the Process of Reading

Note: When slash marks are used, pronounce the letter(s) inside the slash marks (eg. _tub_ is made up of the sounds /t/, /u/, and /b/).

In using _Focus on Phonics_ or any other phonics instructional materials, you need to understand the place of phonics in the process of reading. Much of this section summarizes parts of Chapters 2 and 4 of the report _Applying Research in Reading Instruction for Adults: First Steps for Teachers_ by Susan McShane (Washington, DC: National Institute for Literacy, The Partnership for Reading, 2005), pp. 7–15 and 33–47.

The Process of Reading

The U.S. Congress authorizes the National Institute for Literacy to collect and make available the scientific research on the reading process. Research has identified these components of reading:

- **Alphabetics:** the ability to identify words in print. This term refers to **phonemic awareness**, **decoding**, and sight-word recognition. These terms will be explained in more detail shortly.

- **Fluency:** the ability to identify words rapidly and accurately with little effort.

- **Vocabulary:** the ability to translate printed words into words in readers' speaking vocabularies, to understand the meanings of words used in the text.

- **Comprehension:** the ability to understand the text and also to monitor readers' understanding of what they read. Comprehension is the goal of reading instruction, and all of the components must work together for comprehension to take place.

Phonics instruction such as _Focus on Phonics_ deals especially with the alphabetics component of reading. But as this view of reading makes clear, phonics instruction by itself does not teach people to read. Although _Focus on Phonics_ can help to develop vocabulary, fluency, and comprehension, you will need other materials and strategies that develop these components more directly, since all components are critical to the reading process. Although beginning reading instruction often focuses on the foundational alphabetics skills, the components are not learned sequentially, but together. All the components reinforce each other and often develop simultaneously. Weaknesses in any of the components hinder the ability to read well.

The components of reading listed above can also be categorized as _print-based_ or _meaning-based_ skills. Print-based skills have to do with reading words accurately and rapidly. The components of alphabetics and fluency are _print-based_ skills. If the student can use these skills comfortably and automatically, he can pay attention to the meaning of the text, concentrating on vocabulary and comprehension (which are _meaning-based_ skills). Reading researchers suggest that adults whose meaning skills are significantly stronger than their print skills may have a reading disability. Research also suggests that most reading disabilities are related to reading words quickly. If your student has an adequate speaking vocabulary and can understand material that is read to him but struggles with print-based skills, you may suspect that he has a reading disability or a difficulty related to alphabetics or fluency. (The situation is usually different for ESL learners, who are often skilled in alphabetics and fluency but who have a limited English vocabulary that hinders comprehension.)

A Closer Look at Alphabetics

As noted above, **alphabetics** is the ability to identify words in print. One part of identifying words is recognizing sight words. Sight words are words that readers recognize automatically and read rapidly (that is, they are words that are known immediately on sight). But if your student cannot automatically recognize a word, he must use **decoding** skills to identify it. Decoding skills involve using letter-sound correspondences to figure out unknown words. (Advanced decoding or word analysis skills are used on larger words, such as dividing words into syllables, recognizing prefixes and suffixes, etc.) **Phonics** instruction teaches the relationships between the letters (called _graphemes_) of written language and the individual sounds (called _phonemes_) of spoken language. Students with weak decoding skills need explicit and systematic phonics instruction, such as is provided in _Focus on Phonics_. Your student might first identify a word by decoding, but after many exposures to the same word, the word becomes part of his growing sight vocabulary. Eventually, most words become sight words to a good reader.

For years, teachers taught decoding and phonics skills without considering **phonemic awareness**, without realizing that phonemic awareness was necessary to develop accurate decoding skills. **Phonemic awareness** is about speech sounds only. _Phonemes_ are the smallest units of sound in a spoken language, and phonemic awareness is the ability to detect and manipulate those individual sounds within words.

Phonemic awareness is one part of **phonological awareness**, a broader and more general term that refers to the sounds of speech as distinct from their meanings, and especially the way that spoken language can be subdivided. Phonological awareness ranges from the simplest level (such as being aware of rhyming words), moving up to an awareness of words within sentences, syllables within words, and onsets (initial letter sounds) and rimes (also called _phonograms_, with a vowel and ending consonant sounds; words with the same phonograms can form word patterns that rhyme. For example, in the word *tip*, *t* is the onset and *ip* is the phonogram or rime.) Finally, the most refined and difficult level of phonological awareness is the perception of individual sounds within syllables and words (phonemic awareness).

Teaching Phonemic Awareness

Adults who are good readers may not be aware that they have skills in phonemic awareness or may not remember learning it. Phonemic awareness is not acquired naturally as we learn to speak. Instead, it is usually learned by reading and writing an alphabetic language such as English or Spanish. That's why adult non-readers and very beginning readers have little or no phonemic awareness skills. While they may hear words, they are not aware of the individual phonemes, and they can't answer questions like, "What sound does the word begin with?" or "What vowel sound do you hear in that word?" However, with proper training, most can be taught to identify and manipulate phonemes accurately.

You can assume that all adults who are non-readers or beginning readers lack skills in alphabetics, unless they are learning English as a second or other language. (For ESL learners, the lack of an English vocabulary or other factors may have more to do with their inability to read than their skills in alphabetics.) Students need to learn basic sight words and decoding skills. Why is phonemic awareness a foundational ability necessary for developing decoding skills? It's because when students decode words, they must (1) know and be able to produce the sounds the letters represent, (2) blend those individual sounds as they hear them in sequence, and (3) recognize the words. Phonics training focuses on step 1, but the process may break down in steps 2 and 3 because students lack phonemic awareness.

Not all adults need phonemic awareness training, but many students—even some intermediate adult basic education students—can benefit from it. Students who can use phonics successfully to read and spell words will not need it. But if your students struggle with *Focus on Phonics* or any other phonics materials (that is, if they have difficulty learning the basic sound-symbol relationships taught in phonics instruction or applying those relationships to words they decode), the problem may be that they have not developed skills in phonemic awareness. If so, these skills should be directly taught.

The six phonemic awareness tasks listed below are helpful for instruction and practice. The first two tasks are simpler and may be prerequisites for the more difficult ones.

1. *Phoneme isolation*, which requires recognizing individual sounds in words.

    Examples: "Tell me the first sound in *tall*." [/t/] "Tell me the last sound in *rub*." [/b/]

2. *Phoneme identity*, which requires recognizing the common sound in different words.

    Examples: "Tell me the sound that is the same in *sell*, *soap*, and *sift*." [/s/] "Tell me the sound that is the same in *float*, *bright*, and *gate*." [/t/]

3. *Phoneme categorization*, which requires recognizing the word with the odd sound in a sequence of three or four words.

    Examples: "Which word does not belong: *big, bit, sick, bin?*" [*sick*] "Which word does not belong: *safe, bake, saint, sale?*" [*bake*]

4. *Phoneme blending*, which requires listening to a sequence of separately spoken sounds and combining them to form a recognizable word.

    Examples: "What word is /s/ /p/ /e/ /l/?" [*spell*] "What word is /t/ /a/ /s/ /k/?" [*task*]

5. *Phoneme segmentation*, which requires breaking a word into its sounds by tapping out or counting the sounds or by pronouncing and positioning a marker for each sound.

    Examples: "How many phonemes are there in *wish*?" [three: /w/ /i/ /sh/] "How many phonemes are there in *felt*?" [four: /f/ /e/ /l/ /t/]

6. *Phoneme deletion*, which requires recognizing what word remains when a specified phoneme is removed.

    Examples: "What is *trip* without the /t/?" [rip]. "What is *sent* without the /n/?" [set]

These oral exercises can be done even before a student learns the sound-symbol correspondences that are taught in phonics. If these exercises are too difficult for a student, you can start with simpler tasks that involve larger phonological units like syllables instead of phonemes.

Syllable deletion: "Say *disconnect*." [disconnect]. "Now say it again, but don't say /dis/." [connect]

Syllable identity: "Tell me the syllable that is the same in *careless, careful, uncaring*, and *carefree*." [care]

Syllable blending: "What word is /con/ /fi/ /den/ /tial/?" [confidential]

Syllable segmentation: "How many syllables are there in *respectfully*?" [four: /re/ /spect/ /ful/ /ly/]

Syllable deletion: "What is independent without the /in/?" [dependent]

Doing oral exercises with each of the different phonemic awareness tasks (first with syllables if necessary, and then with phonemes) can be helpful both for assessing students' abilities and for instruction. You may want to focus on one or two types of phonemic awareness tasks at a time. Phonemic awareness is not an end in itself. You teach it when and for as long as it takes for students to manipulate the sounds that enable them to use phonics in reading and

174

spelling. In fact, it is best to teach phonemic awareness along with phonics. Research shows that using letters to teach phonemic awareness is more effective than doing oral practice alone. You can have students write letters or manipulate letter cards as they produce the sounds the letters represent. You may want to build in some phonemic awareness practice that highlights whatever sound(s) the student is studying in *Focus on Phonics*.

Phonemic segmenting and blending, two of the more difficult phonemic awareness tasks, are especially helpful to teach to students. That's because students use phonemic blending to sound out words and use phonemic segmenting to decide how words are spelled. Do not expect students to have perfect phonemic awareness before they work on phonics and decoding skills; some students may never be able to do the most difficult phoneme manipulation, but they can still make some progress with phonics and decoding. As students become skilled in phonemic awareness and decoding, they will be able to read increasingly more difficult material.

Decoding skills, important as they are, do not work alone. As readers focus on comprehension, they should test whether the words they have decoded make sense in what they read. That is, students should use both decoding skills and context clues to figure out unknown words. Beginning readers tend to focus primarily on recognizing or figuring out unknown words in the text. If the words are in their speaking vocabularies and they can decode them, they can usually understand the text. More advanced readers also encounter unfamiliar words, but their task is different; they usually can decode a word but don't know what it means. They may pronounce the word and then use context clues from the text or use a dictionary to find out what the word means.

Finally, keep in mind that the direct skills instruction of *Focus on Phonics* should not be the only focus of the reading lesson. You need to help students develop not just alphabetics skills but also skills in fluency, vocabulary, and comprehension. It is best to use some meaningful, authentic (real-life) materials that interest students and that relate to their work and home lives. If these interesting materials are too difficult for students to read independently, you can make recordings of the materials for students to listen to and read along with. You may want to have students dictate their own stories and let those stories become the main reading material (the language experience approach). And you may want to have students make their own word banks or personal dictionaries to build their vocabularies. These strategies make reading lessons more enjoyable and build skills in all the reading components: alphabetics, fluency, vocabulary, and comprehension.

Appendix B: Using This Workbook with Groups

Most teachers or tutors will use this workbook one-to-one with a student. But suppose you want to use it with a group of students or a whole class. And suppose you want some students to do the same practice at the same time. Before you have a group of two or more students work on a single practice, make sure the answer to these questions is yes:

1. Does each student need to do the practice?

2. Does each student have the necessary background, sight vocabulary, and skills to do the practice?

3. Can you help each student discover sound-symbol relationships for himself? (The student should not just be getting answers or checking his work.)

4. Can the students work well together? Will each actively participate?

5. Can each student—especially the less able ones—experience success? Are you sure no students will be frustrated or embarrassed, especially if they take turns? Can you give help to students before, during, or after they do the practice?

If you have only two or three students doing the same practice, you can probably work in a small group. But if you have more, they may have trouble following along with you in their individual workbooks. In that case, you can copy parts of the practice on the board or make transparencies to use with an overhead projector. Then several students can follow along with you by looking at the practice on the board or the screen. You may need to speak louder and more distinctly to be heard in a group. And feel free to change the suggested dialog to fit the group situation.

Do you want your students to take turns answering? If so, note any students who have trouble answering on their own. You can spare them embarrassment by calling only on students who volunteer answers. Or you can have the whole group of students read in unison, or repeat words after you read them. Make sure to check individually with students who don't participate much. Ask if you are going too fast or if they need extra help.

Do you need teaching materials you can use in groups? You and your students may want to make your own teaching materials, using the content in this workbook. A few examples: Put the workbook vocabulary words on flash cards and match the words with pictures, make the words into sentences, put the words together to form compound words, or use the cards in a game you make up. Make word wheels using word-family words or words with the same or different endings. Create Bingo games or other board games with sight vocabulary words or word-family words. There are many other possibilities!

Now suppose you are using this workbook with many students, but each student is working on a different practice. Besides using aides or helpers to assist students, how can you individualize instruction? One way you can give individual exercises to many students at the same time is to record audio of the practices on tape, CD, or computer file. Each student can then do his own practice while listening to the audio for that practice. This system has many advantages. A student can do a practice when he is most ready for it. He can work by himself while you and other students may be doing something entirely different. A student can work at his own pace, skipping parts of the audio, stopping when he wants to, or going over some parts again. He can work on the practice anywhere, and he may even be able to take the recording with him to do as homework. Finally, the student can spend time with you working on other materials. If some students are listening to audio in the classroom, they should use earphones or headphones to cut down on the noise.

All of the practices except the endings practices could be recorded. It is better for students to do the endings practices in class while you dictate because these practices have a lot of spelling and writing, and you must check the student's work several times throughout the practice.

Your voice should sound very clear and distinct on any audio recording you make. Bad recordings are worse than no recordings! You can plan the format for each type of practice yourself, and your dialog may differ from the suggested dialog. As you make the audio recording, think: Will the student need time to repeat words? To read words and sentences by himself? To write words? If so, you should allow long pauses, use a tape recorder with a pause mechanism, or have the student stop the recording. Do you plan to give the answers on the recording and let the student correct his own errors? Or will you go over his completed practice sheet and correct it? If you are working with a student who really needs your help, you may want to do the practice one-to-one with him, but send him home with a recording of the sentences. He can reread the sentences at home, reading each sentence before he hears it. ["Sentence number 1." (long pause for student to read) (you read the sentence once or twice)] Or the student can put the book away and use the audio for writing practice. ["Sentence number 1." (you read the sentence twice, then pause)]. The student can stop or pause the recording and write the sentence, resuming the audio for the next sentence. He can later check his work by comparing the sentences he wrote with the ones in the workbook. Since much time is often required to have a student write all or most of the sentences, it can be very helpful for him to do this at home.

Here is one more suggestion for the student who has finished part or all of the workbook. Encourage him to write stories using the workbook vocabulary and perhaps some other words he has learned. You can type these stories and reproduce them for the rest of the class. The stories not only become a source of pride for the writer, they are also useful for individualizing instruction, giving several students practice with the workbook vocabulary.

Have fun thinking up other ways to use this workbook in your class.

Appendix C: Helping Students Decode Words with Blends

Words with blends are often difficult for students to decode. It is important that they have a good knowledge of both consonant sounds and short vowel sounds before doing Part B of this workbook. If you discover that students need more help with consonant or vowel sounds as they start Part B, give them more practice before beginning to decode words with blends.

Many students have trouble decoding words (with or without blends) because they lack phonemic awareness skills. These skills are foundational to using phonics skills. If students have trouble with Part A of this workbook or if they seems to struggle with phonics materials or with decoding words, refer to Appendix A: Phonics, Phonemic Awareness, and the Process of Reading. This Appendix will give you ideas about how to help students build phonemic awareness skills if necessary.

As Appendix A notes, blending is one of the most difficult of the phonemic awareness skills. Blending sounds together is essential to decoding words for reading. Examples of blending exercises in Appendix A may be helpful. For students who have difficulty with blending sounds together in general, you may want to have them practice blending sounds by giving the students individual sounds, just a moment apart, to blend. If you do this, avoid attaching any vowel sounds to the individual consonant sounds. If necessary, you can demonstrate this by blending some sounds yourself and having students repeat after you.

Students may find words with consonant blends more challenging because the consonant sounds come so close together. In the blends practices, words are always grouped together by similar beginning or ending blends. To introduce sounding out the blend, two words are used. For beginning blends, the first letter of the blend is added to the first word to make the second word (e.g., *rag/brag*). So the student discovers, for example, how the beginning blend /br/ differs from the consonant sound /r/ in words. You may want to give students more examples and practice with word pairs like these. Or, if they still seem unsure of the sound of the blend, you may try contrasting the other consonant sounds in word pairs—by comparing *brag* with *bag*, for example. For most of the ending blends, the last letter of the blend is added to the first word to make the second word (e.g., *ban/band*). You may want to compare the blend with the other consonant sound (compare *band* with *bad*, for example). This kind of practice may help students learn and recognize the blend sounds better.

If a student has learned a beginning or ending blend well, he should consistently pronounce it correctly in the word lists. His next task is to blend the sounds with other beginning or ending sounds and a short vowel sound in words. If this is difficult, have the student blend the sounds in the way he can do it best, ignoring the practice dialog. A student working on the ending blend *-nd*, for example, may combine the *a* and *-nd* into an ending stem /and/ and then try to blend beginning consonant sounds with /and/. Or he may blend the beginning sound(s) and the /a/ sound first, and then add the blend /nd/ to the end. Or he may try to pronounce each sound individually, blending the sounds together into a word. You can explore with each student the methods of decoding that work best.

If a student knows and can pronounce the individual sounds in the word but substitutes some different sounds when he blends them together, he may have a problem with auditory memory. He may have difficulty remembering the sounds or remembering their order in a word. Another common decoding problem, especially with blend words, is reversing the order of some sounds (e.g., *ruts* for *rust*, *trap* for *tarp*, or *stop* for *spot*). For all of these problems, you might help the student by writing down the sounds that he actually says. Then he can see how he has put together the sounds in a word and can compare it with how it should be sounded out. This process can pinpoint troublesome words or parts of words, or can suggest different methods the student can use in decoding words.

Finally, with some students you may want to avoid a phonetic approach altogether. These students find it easier to learn words as wholes. They have difficulty learning words by breaking them down and sounding them out, or by blending sounds together. For these students, you might want to try other techniques, such as kinesthetic tracing.

Foreign students and students with certain dialects may have special difficulties with blend words. For references outlining sounds foreign students may have trouble with, see *Pronunciation Contrasts in English* by Don L. F. Nilsen and Alleen Pace Nilsen (Waveland Press, 2002), and Chapter 15, "Consonant Clusters," in *Manual of American English Pronunciation*, 4th ed., by Clifford H. Prator, Jr., and Betty Wallace Robinett (Harcourt College Publications, 1985). For an excellent analysis of Black English which includes a discussion of pronunciation features teachers should be aware of, see the chapter "Some Linguistic Features of Negro Dialect" by Ralph W. Fasold and Walt Wolfram, in *Black American English, Its Background and Its Usage in the Schools and in Literature*, edited by Paul Stoller (New York: Dell Publishing Co., 1975.).

Appendix D: Creating Your Own Exercises for Word Endings

In *Laubach Way to Reading 2* and in Part A of this workbook, the student has had practice with the endings *-s, -ing, -y,* and *-er.* There was more limited practice with endings *-es, -ies, -ed,* and *-ier.* There are no endings practices in Part B of this workbook, but you are encouraged to make up your own endings exercises for the endings you want your student to practice.

You may want to make exercises each time the student finishes a group of blends, using the blend words the student has just studied. (Blend words with *-y* and *-er* are in Appendixes E and F respectively, in the order the blends appear in this book.)

This appendix can give you some ideas for exercises. In the sample exercises below, the *-s* ending is used on words that are both nouns and verbs. The *-er* ending can mean either "a person or thing that does something" or "more." The endings *-ing, -ed, -er,* and *-y* are used on words in which the last consonant of the root word is doubled (words ending with Consonant-Vowel-Consonant) and where it is not doubled (words ending with Vowel-Consonant-Consonant). And the *-ing, -ed,* and *-er* endings are also used on words ending with *e.*

In your exercises, you may want to cover only certain endings and certain types of words (for example, words in which the last consonant is doubled before adding the ending). Or, you may mix several endings or types of words together, depending on what your student should practice.

Often, students need many more exercises to get enough practice with endings. Be sure your student knows the blend words that you plan to use in the exercise well.

178

Appendix E: Words with -y Endings

In this Appendix and Appendix F, the words are grouped in the order in which their roots appear in the book. Sight words introduced in the practices are also listed. The groups are separated in this way to make it easier for the teacher to have the student practice the -y and -er endings after finishing each blend group.

Words in which the root word ends with e have an asterisk (*) in front of them. For these words, the e is dropped before the -y ending is added. If the student has not studied -y endings on words that end with e, you may want to point out these words.

The ending -y is often added to nouns or verbs to make adjectives. The ending -y can mean *full of, like, somewhat,* or *having* as in *dirty, crabby, chilly,* and *classy.*

Key to Grouping of Words

I. Review of Beginning and Ending Digraphs
II. Beginning Blends with *l*
III. Beginning Blends with *r*
IV. Beginning Blends with *s* and *w*

V. Beginning Three-letter Blends
VI. Review of Beginning Blends
VII. Ending Blends with *n*
VIII. Other Ending Blends
IX. Vowels + *r*

-y words in which last consonant of root word is *not* doubled:

I	II	III	IV	V	VII	VIII		IX	
chilly	blotchy	brassy	sticky	stretchy	minty	bumpy	risky	jerky	corny
catchy	classy	cranky	stinky	stringy	handy	dumpy	husky	perky	thorny
patchy	flashy	dressy	stocky	scratchy	sandy	lumpy	crispy	*nervy	shorty
itchy	fleshy	frilly	stuffy	springy	windy	misty	guilty	whirly	sporty
fishy	fluffy	grassy	smelly		crunchy	dusty	milky	squirmy	stormy
	plucky	trashy	*smudgy		*chancy	gusty	silky	dirty	pearly
	glassy	tricky	sketchy		springy	musty	crafty	thirsty	earthy
	slushy				stringy	rusty	drafty	curly	wordy
					stinky	crusty	shifty	*curvy	wormy
					junky	trusty	thrifty	hardy	worthy
						pesty		marshy	
						testy		starchy	

-y words in which last consonant of root word *is* doubled:

I	II	III	IV	V	IX
chatty	clammy	bratty	spotty	scrappy	furry
choppy	floppy	crabby	snappy		blurry
		drippy	snobby		starry
		grabby	smoggy		
		gritty	skinny		
		grubby			

Appendix F: Words with *-er* Endings

Please read the first paragraph of Appendix C. It applies to this Appendix also.
Words with an asterisk (*) are those in which the root words end with an *e,* and only an *r* is added for the *-er* ending.

Agent Nouns: In these words, the *-er* usually means *a person or thing that does something.*

***-er* words in which last consonant of the root word is *not* doubled:**

I	II	drinker	V	sender	stinger	bumper	golfer	turner	*forger
shocker	blinker	player	stretcher	blender	swinger	jumper	lifter	burner	earner
checker	blocker	trucker	scratcher	spender	banker	stumper	sifter	marker	learner
thinker	blusher		thriller	sander	tanker	twister	drifter	charmer	searcher
whistler	flasher	IV		rancher	sinker	duster		farmer	worker
catcher	flicker	sticker	VII	quencher	thinker	tester	IX	gardener	
pitcher		stringer	planter	puncher	drinker	husker	herder	charter	
dasher	III	stinker	renter	*dancer	stinker	crisper	merger	starter	
masher	cracker	stuffer	printer	*plunger		welder	server	marcher	
	crasher	speller	hunter	hanger	VIII	builder	twirler	*lover	
	crusher	swinger	punter	ringer	camper	scalper	surfer	sorter	
	dresser		lender	singer	damper	helper	curler	scorcher	

***-er* words in which last consonant of root word *is* doubled:**

I	II	III	IV	V
shipper	blotter	dropper	stopper	stripper
shopper	clapper	drummer	spinner	scrubber
shutter	clipper	trapper	snapper	shredder
chatter	flapper	trimmer	scanner	
chopper	flipper	trotter	swimmer	
	planner			
	slipper			
	slugger			

Comparative Adjectives: In these words, the *-er* means *more.*

***-er* words in which last consonant of the root word is *not* doubled:**

I	II	III	IV	VII	VIII	IX	smarter
thicker	blacker	drunker	stiffer	fonder	damper	firmer	harsher
richer	sticker	fresher	smarter		faster	darker	newer
fresher					crisper	larger	shorter
					swifter	harder	
					stricter	sharper	

***-er* words in which last consonant of root word *is* doubled:**

I	II
thinner	flatter
	slimmer

Appendix G: Compound Words

All of the compound words in this list are made up of words that the student has learned in this *Laubach Way to Reading* and *Focus on Phonics* levels 1 and 2..

aftermath	downcast	hangover	newsprint	patchwork	slingshot	thanksgiving	wellspring
anything	downwind	hardback	newsstand	pigskin	snapshot	turnabout	wetland
armpit	dropout	hardcover	northwest	pinworm	something	turnout	windbag
backdrop	drumstick	hardtop	offhand	pitchfork	spendthrift	turnover	windburn
backhand	dustpan	headband	oneself	plaything	splashdown	underarm	windchill
backtrack	earthworm	headdress	outburst	popcorn	sportscast	underbrush	windmill
bandstand	eggplant	headfirst	outcast	printout	sportsman	undercover	windstorm
barnyard	everything	herself	outlast	quicksand	sportswoman	underhand	windswept
birdbath	farmhand	himself	outrank	rattrap	standby	underpants	wingspan
birthday	farmland	horseback	outsmart	redwing	standoff	undershirt	witchcraft
birthmark	filmstrip	humdrum	outstanding	ringworm	standstill	undershorts	workbench
blackbird	fingerprint	inchworm	overspend	riverbank	starfish	understand	workday
blackjack	firstborn	inkblot	overstock	sandbag	stepbrother	understudy	workhorse
blacklist	firsthand	itself	overstrict	sandbar	stepfather	underworld	workman
blacksmith	flashback	kickstand	overact	sandblast	stepmother	upbringing	yardstick
blacktop	forklift	kingpin	overcast	sandman	stepson	upbuild	yourself
blockhead	gangland	landfill	overdraft	sandpaper	stinkbug	upland	
breadbasket	grandchildren	landmark	overhand	sandstorm	stockyard	uplift	
buckskin	grandfather	leftover	overhang	sharkskin	stopgap	upstanding	
carport	grandmother	lipstick	overhead	shipyard	stopwatch	upstart	
chopstick	grandstand	locksmith	overheard	shoplift	streetcar	upswing	
clockwork	grillwork	lovebird	overland	shopworn	sunburn	upturn	
cornstarch	hairbrush	manhunt	overturn	shortcut	sunburst	upwind	
crabgrass	hamstring	markdown	overwork	shorthand	sunglasses	watchband	
crackdown	handbag	milkman	packhorse	shortstop	sunlamp	watchword	
crackpot	handstand	myself	passport	silkworm	sunspot	watercolor	
dipstick	hangman	newscast	password	skinflint	switchman	watermark	

Appendix H: Words That End with *CC-le*

This list includes words from Practice 53A-B, plus some other words that you may wish to introduce to your student.

-bble	-ffle	-ssle	-ckle	-ncle	-mple	-stle
babble	baffle	hassle	cackle	uncle	ample	castle
dabble	raffle	tussle	crackle		sample	nestle
pebble	sniffle		tackle		trample	bristle
dribble	muffle		freckle		temple	gristle
nibble	ruffle	**-ttle**	heckle	**-ngle**	dimple	thistle
scribble	scuffle	battle	speckle	angle	pimple	whistle
gobble	shuffle	cattle	pickle	dangle	simple	bustle
wobble		rattle	sickle	jangle	crumple	hustle
bubble		tattle	tickle	mangle		rustle
	-ggle	kettle	trickle	strangle		
-ddle	giggle	settle	buckle	tangle	**-mble**	
paddle	jiggle	brittle	chuckle	jingle	gamble	**r-C-le**
saddle	wiggle	little		mingle	ramble	marble
straddle	juggle	whittle		shingle	scramble	curdle
meddle	smuggle	bottle		single	tremble	girdle
peddle	snuggle	throttle	**-ndle**	tingle	thimble	hurdle
fiddle	struggle	shuttle	candle	jungle	bumble	sparkle
griddle			handle		crumble	startle
middle		**-zzle**	kindle		fumble	circle
riddle		dazzle	spindle		grumble	gargle
coddle	**-pple**	drizzle	swindle	**-nkle**	humble	gurgle
toddle	apple	fizzle	bundle	ankle	jumble	purple
cuddle	cripple	sizzle		crinkle	mumble	turtle
huddle	nipple	nozzle		sprinkle	rumble	
muddle	ripple	guzzle	**-ntle**	tinkle	stumble	
puddle	topple	muzzle	gentle	twinkle	tumble	
		puzzle	mantle			

182